John Brown

LEADERS OF THE CIVIL WAR ERA

John Brown

Jefferson Davis

Frederick Douglass

Ulysses S. Grant

Stonewall Jackson

Robert E. Lee

Abraham Lincoln

William Tecumseh Sherman

Harriet Beecher Stowe

Harriet Tubman

LEADERS OF THE CIVIL WAR ERA

John Brown

Jon Sterngass

CHELSEA HOUSE
PUBLISHERS
An imprint of Infobase Publishing

JOHN BROWN

Chelsea House
An imprint of Infobase Publishing
132 West 31st Street
New York NY 10001

Library of Congress Cataloging-in-Publication Data
Sterngass, Jon.
John Brown / Jon Sterngass.
    p. cm. — (Leaders of the Civil War era)
Includes bibliographical references and index.
ISBN 978-1-60413-305-9 (hardcover)
1. Brown, John, 1800–1859—Juvenile literature. 2. Abolitionists—United States—Biography—Juvenile literature. 3. Antislavery movements—United States—History—19th century—Juvenile literature. I. Title. II. Series.
E451.S855 2009
973.7'116092—dc22
[B]   2008044622

Chelsea House books are available at special discounts when purchased in bulk quantities for businesses, associations, institutions, or sales promotions. Please call our Special Sales Department in New York at (212) 967-8800 or (800) 322-8755.

You can find Chelsea House on the World Wide Web at http://www.chelseahouse.com

Series design by Erik Lindstrom
Cover design and composition by Keith Trego
 Cover printed by Yurchak Printing, Landisville, Pa.
Book printed and bound by Yurchak Printing, Landisville, Pa.

Printed in the United States of America

CONTENTS

Hard to Tell Who's Mad

John Brown (1800–1859) was a white American abolitionist who led a raid on Harpers Ferry, Virginia (now West Virginia), in 1859. In this raid, Brown and his 21 men achieved some early successes in their war to abolish slavery. They managed to seize the U.S. arsenal, where thousands of weapons were stored. Brown hoped enslaved blacks would rise up and support his invasion. He wanted to establish a free state in the Appalachian Mountains where slaves could find refuge. He believed that his raid might lead to the collapse of slavery in the South. However, the attack failed. Within 36 hours, all of Brown's men were either fleeing for their lives, lying dead in Harpers Ferry, or had become captives of the government of Virginia.

Yet this was not the end of the story. Brown survived the raid. He was tried by the state of Virginia for murder and treason.

John Brown has been called one of "the most controversial of all nineteenth-century Americans" because of his crusade to end slavery, by any means necessary. Brown was an active supporter of the Underground Railroad, helped to establish an organization to protect fugitive slaves from their captors, and treated blacks as his equal. He also was very violent; he was responsible for the cold-blooded massacre of five settlers in a proslavery town.

His courageous behavior at the trial seemed heroic to millions of Americans. Brown's eloquent condemnations of slavery and his defense of his actions captivated the nation. When Virginia hanged him, only a month after his raid, Brown became a martyr to the antislavery cause.

Brown's Harpers Ferry raid increased tensions between the North and the South. It helped convince many white Southerners that leaving the United States was the only way they could protect their way of life based around slavery. Only 16 months after the raid on Harpers Ferry, the American Civil War began, in April 1861.

John Brown is a controversial American. The evaluation of his character, motives, impact, and meaning continues to stir passionate debate. Brown was a bundle of contradictions; he possessed noble virtues as well as great failings. He could be gentle as well as violent, sometimes calm and occasionally angry, humble and then self-righteous, empathetic and apathetic. His willingness to use violence to abolish slavery made him an unusual white person in the mid-1800s. To some, he was a selfless martyr, a new saint, and a symbol of the possibilities of a color-blind United States. Others criticized Brown, calling him a lunatic and a terrorist, a business failure and a cold-blooded murderer. Thomas Wentworth Higginson, one of Brown's backers, once commented that there were "few elements in the tale of Harpers Ferry that are strictly either black or white. Most elements of the story . . . are quite gray."

One issue that does not appear to be "gray" to twenty-first-century eyes is the evils of slavery. Slavery was an immoral institution that needed to be eliminated from American society. Yet to a large degree, slave labor built the prosperity of the United States. The social and economic system of the Southern United States depended on the slave system. At the time of the American Revolution, many white Americans thought of slavery as a necessary evil that would pass away in time. But it did not happen that way. By the time of Brown's raid on Harpers Ferry, there were 4 million enslaved African Americans in the United States. In 1859, the United States was one of the last and largest slaveholding societies in Europe or the Americas.

SLAVERY AND COTTON

For hundreds of years, most Europeans wore clothes made from wool or flax. Cotton spinning and weaving were very small industries. In the late 1700s, however, the Industrial Revolution began in Europe. New machines made it easy to produce cotton textiles cheaply and in large amounts. Soon there was a tremendous demand for cotton to feed the new machines.

In 1790, the entire United States produced only 3,000 bales of cotton. Cotton grew well in many areas of the South, but there was one big problem. The seeds were so difficult to remove from the fiber that it took an entire day to hand clean a single pound of cotton. In the 1790s, a number of inventors, including Eli Whitney, developed a machine to separate the seeds from the fiber of cotton. The cotton gin (short for "engine") was simply a hand-cranked cylinder with metal teeth. However, the cotton gin made it possible to clean 50 pounds of cotton a day.

Thousands of whites moved into the interior of South Carolina and Georgia to grow cotton using black slaves as workers. By 1811, this area was producing 60 million pounds of cotton a year. White farmers then rushed into Alabama and Mississippi with their black slaves. Only 50 years later, the southern United States grew 60 percent of the world's cotton.

So slavery did not die out in the United States. In fact, the number of slaves grew tremendously and the South became a slave society. In 1860, about one third of all Southern white families owned slaves. Many others hoped to own them. Powerful slave owners dominated politics, the courts, and the sheriff's office in the South. This system was known as a plantocracy. At the same time, for many different reasons, slavery had completely died out in the North.

MISERY FOR AFRICAN AMERICANS

For white Americans, growing cotton meant opportunity. For enslaved blacks, it meant misery. Whites uprooted thousands of African Americans from the Chesapeake or Carolina regions

With the invention of the cotton gin in 1793—a machine that allowed cotton fibers and seeds to be separated quicker and easier—came the call for more workers to labor in the cotton fields. Due to the promise of increased profits, hundreds of thousands of black men and women were enslaved in order to plant, chop, and pick cotton.

and forced them to move west. At any time, slave families could be separated and children sold away. About one out of every four African-American families was broken up by the sale of a family member. By 1860, almost a million American slaves had been moved against their will from the place of their birth to the booming cotton states.

Enslaved blacks on cotton plantations often worked from dawn to dusk, and sometimes longer. Slaves cleared the land, tended the crops, and built the houses. Household slaves cooked, cleaned, and took care of the master's children. Of course, enslaved African Americans were not paid for their work. Their labor, and their lives, were literally stolen by their white masters. Slave women had to endure sexual exploitation and rape. They often bore the children of their masters and overseers. Masters disciplined slaves by whipping, imprisonment, torture, and mutilation. Southern laws considered enslaved human beings as property.

Life for free blacks in the South was not much better. They enjoyed none of the civil rights written in the Bill of Rights. They could not vote or testify against a white person in court. Even in the North, the rights of free blacks were severely restricted. This was life for one out of every seven people in the "free republic."

WHO WAS SANE?

Many opponents of John Brown claimed he was insane. Yet if Brown had been black, no one would have considered him mad. He might have been called extreme, fanatical, enraged, desperate, reckless . . . but not crazy. The distinction reveals the importance of skin color in American history. Many Americans could easily justify a black man who fought and died to help free the slaves and win black people's rights to life, liberty, and the pursuit of happiness. Yet a white man who did this must have been crazy.

Brown was deeply sensitive to injustice. He felt tremendous sympathy for black people in the United States. Brown believed that slavery was a sin against God. He was extremely disturbed that a nation, which claimed to be both Christian and free, should tolerate, let alone support, slavery. Brown willingly devoted himself to an extremely unpopular cause. He gave up his own chances of personal gain in order to ease the suffering of others. He saw himself as a revolutionary, called by God to a special destiny.

Brown lived at a time when white people held 4 million African Americans in bondage, yet most white Americans justified this system. They called slavery a positive good and said it was justified by the Bible. They invented ridiculous scientific explanations for the benefits of slavery and the inferiority of African Americans. Even white Americans who did not own slaves seemed indifferent to the horrors of slavery. They considered the United States the land of the free and the home of the brave.

One of Brown's men put it best. Just before the Harpers Ferry raid, he wrote, "Millions of fellow beings require it of us; their cries for help go out to the universe daily and hourly. Whose duty is it to help them? Is it yours, is it mine? It is every man's, but how few there are to help. . . . If my life is sacrificed, it can't be lost in a better cause."

Who was sane—the people who owned other human beings and treated them like cattle or the people who fought the system? As the abolitionist Wendell Phillips declared, "Call them madmen if you will," but in a slave-oriented society, it was "hard to tell who's mad." From the distance of a century and a half later, the choice does not seem quite as difficult. Despite Brown's many faults, he now seems far more rational than those Americans who practiced and accepted the inhumanity of slavery.

DID JOHN BROWN FAIL?

Frederick Douglass, the great African-American speaker, writer, and abolitionist, was a good friend of Brown's. After the Civil War, which ended slavery at the cost of 600,000 American lives, Douglass wrote a lecture memorializing the Harpers Ferry raid. Douglass delivered the lecture, entitled "Did John Brown Fail?" many times across the United States. Douglass's lecture concluded with this upbeat assessment of Brown's place in American history:

> If John Brown did not end the war that ended slavery, he did at least begin the war that ended slavery. . . . Until this blow was struck, the prospect for freedom was dim, shadowy, and uncertain. The irrepressible conflict was one of words, votes, and compromises. When John Brown stretched forth his arm, the sky was cleared. The time for compromises was gone—the armed hosts of freedom stood face to face over the chasm of a broken Union—and the clash of arms was at hand. The South staked all upon getting possession of the Federal Government, and failing to do that, drew the sword of rebellion and thus made her own, and not Brown's, the lost cause of the century.

The Businessman

John Brown was born on May 9, 1800, in Torrington, Connecticut. He was the fourth of eight children of Owen Brown and Ruth Mills. The Brown family had lived in New England for almost 200 years. Both John Brown's father and his grandfather had fought in the American Revolution. Still, Owen Brown believed he could make a better life for his family if he moved westward. When John was five years old, the Browns moved from Connecticut to Hudson, a rough settlement in northeastern Ohio.

Owen was a tanner, someone who treats skins and hides with tannic acid in order to change them into leather. In 1808, disaster struck. Owen's wife, Ruth, and a baby daughter both died during childbirth. Realizing that he could not raise six children on his own, Owen found a wife within the year. At the age of 39, Owen married Sally Root, who was 18. The changes stunned the eight-year-old John, who was still grieving the death of his mother. He never really got along with his stepmother. He later recalled that he "continued to pine after his own mother for years."

Before 1812, European-Americans were still a minority in Ohio. Unlike many whites in the Midwest, young John made friends with several American Indians. He remembered that he "used to hang about with them quite as much as was consistent with good manners; and learned a trifle of their talk."

As a child, John loved to play outdoors. He rambled across the undeveloped countryside, looking for birds, squirrels, and if he was lucky, a wild turkey's nest. John admitted he was very "fond of the hardest and roughest kind of plays; and could never get enough. . . ." John did not like going to school; instead he preferred "to wrestle and snow ball and run and jump and knock off old seed wool hats." He also loved to read, especially history. He later claimed that reading "diverted him in a great measure from bad company."

From his father, John learned to dress leather from squirrel and raccoon skins. He made "whip lashes," which he sold for pocket money. John loved to work with leather and was proud of his developing skill as a tanner.

RELIGIOUS BELIEFS

John also adopted his father's religious beliefs. Owen, a Protestant Christian known as a Calvinist, saw God as less of a friend and more of a judge. The Browns worried constantly about the afterlife and their household echoed with the sounds of prayers and Bible readings. Owen taught John to "fear God and keep his commandments." Owen was a strict disciplinarian and believed in corporal punishment. John would grow up to raise his family in a similar way.

John Brown and his family were followers of Calvinism. Calvinism is a religious system and approach to a Christian life that emphasizes the rule of God above all things. Pictured is John Calvin, one of the most influential leaders of the Protestant Reformation movement.

John's father hated slavery and taught his family that holding human beings as slaves was a sin against God. Throughout his life, Owen was involved in antislavery activities and John followed his example.

During the War of 1812, Owen won a contract to provide beef to American forces near Detroit. He gave John, who was 12 years old, the job of gathering the cattle and driving them more than 100 miles to Michigan. Upon arriving in Michigan, John stayed with a man who owned a boy slave. The man beat the slave with an iron shovel right in front of John. Brown later wrote that watching the beating of the slave transformed him into "a most determined abolitionist . . . leading him to declare, or swear: eternal war with slavery."

BE PERFECT

In about 1800, a Christian movement known as the Second Great Awakening began to spread across the United States. Preachers such as Charles Finney emphasized a very personal relationship with a friendly God. They taught that human beings have free choice in moral decisions. They also believed in the possibility of divine forgiveness for all people. In many areas, "camp meeting"-style preaching drew thousands of people. The Second Great Awakening made extremely emotional displays of religious belief more common.

The Second Great Awakening also contributed to the growing reform movements of the era. Americans tried to put their religious principles in action in order to change society for the better. They took their inspiration from the conclusion to the Sermon on the Mount in Matthew 5:48,

(continues)

(continued)

when Jesus says, "You must, therefore, be perfect as your heavenly Father is perfect."

Many Christian Americans of the early 1800s took this literally. They were called perfectionists. They believed that people should try to perfect themselves and society by doing as much good as they possibly could. These new beliefs attracted thousands of people in New England, New York, and Ohio. The spirit of the Second Great Awakening led to reform movements such as antislavery, women's rights, temperance, and prison reform.

John Brown did not like much of the preaching of the Second Great Awakening. The new beliefs ran contrary to his Calvinist-influenced view of the world. Brown's religion lacked the sense of joyfulness and optimism that were basic to the beliefs of many other abolitionists. Still, no white person was more opposed to slavery than John Brown.

AN INDEPENDENT LIFE

At the age of 16, John left his family and went to Plainfield, Massachusetts, to prepare for college and eventually to study to be a minister. Shortly afterward, he transferred to the Morris Academy in Litchfield, Connecticut. Soon, John's money ran out and he developed severe eye problems from studying for long hours by candlelight. He was forced to give up his studies at the academy and return to Ohio.

In Ohio, John worked briefly at his father's tannery and then opened his own tannery outside of town. As the tannery prospered, he hired a woman and her daughter to do the cooking. He thought the younger woman, Dianthe Lusk, was a "neat, industrious and economical girl, of excellent character and remarkable piety." They married in 1820 and their first child was born 13 months later. They eventually had seven children together; only five of them—John Jr., Jason, Owen, Ruth, and Frederick—lived to adulthood.

For the next 12 years, Brown lived a fairly typical frontier life with Dianthe. He concerned himself mainly with providing for his growing family and succeeding in business. In 1825, Brown and his family moved to New Richmond, Pennsylvania, where he bought 200 acres of land. He cleared 25 acres and built a cabin, a barn, and a tannery for leather production. Within a year, the tannery employed 15 men. Brown also made money raising cattle and surveying, a skill that he had taught himself. He was a model citizen and helped to establish a post office and a school for the town.

Brown was a fine tanner, but he never had the head for the business. He loved dealing with sheep and cattle because it gave him a chance to work around animals. As a result, he developed a close connection to some of the figures he read about in the Bible.

Brown began to face hard times. In 1831, one of his sons died, and Brown also became ill. His businesses began to suffer, leaving him with considerable debt. In the summer of 1832, Dianthe died due to complications following childbirth. The death of his wife left Brown severely depressed. He wrote to a business partner, "I find that I am still getting more and more unfit for everything. I have been growing numb for a good while."

Like his father, Brown was left to raise his children alone. His children needed a mother and running the tannery was strenuous work. On June 14, 1833, the 33-year-old Brown married 16-year-old Mary Ann Day, the daughter of a local blacksmith from Meadville, Pennsylvania. They eventually had 13 children together, in addition to the 7 children from his previous marriage.

Pictured is Mary Ann Day (1817-1884), Brown's second wife, with daughters Anne, left, and Sarah, c1851. Mary was a hard worker, which Brown admired. Too bashful to ask for her hand directly, Brown presented her with a written offer of marriage. They were married June 14, 1833.

Brown's economic hardships increased as he attempted to provide for his expanding family. Of Brown's 20 children, only 8 (4 by each wife) would outlive him. Two died shortly after being born, six died of childhood illnesses, and one was scalded to death in a kitchen accident. Three of Brown's adult sons would die in the Harpers Ferry raid.

HARD TIMES

In 1836, Brown left his property in Pennsylvania and moved his family to Franklin Mills (present-day Kent), Ohio. In this part of the state, known as the Western Reserve, many people bought land for speculation purposes. Brown built and operated a tannery along the Cuyahoga River. A number of investors believed that Franklin Mills was going to turn into a major industrial city. The Pennsylvania and Ohio Canal, stretching from Pittsburgh to Cleveland, would run right through the town.

Like many others, Brown believed that real estate in Franklin Mills was going to be extremely valuable. Farms in the county had recently risen 100 percent in value. Town lots in Akron, Cleveland, and Cuyahoga Falls now sold at unbelievably high prices. Borrowed money (known as credit) was easy to obtain in Ohio at the time. Brown borrowed a lot of money, bought almost 100 acres of land, and waited for his investment to pay off.

Instead, the U.S. economy collapsed. The economic crisis was known as the Panic of 1837. Franklin Mills never developed into a major city, and Brown's creditors demanded the repayment of their loans. Brown suffered great financial losses, and lawsuits against him piled up. In fact, at one point, Brown had no money to afford postage for a letter. His large family hardly knew where their next meal would come from.

Brown attempted several different business schemes in an effort to get out of debt. In addition to tanning hides and trading in cattle, he also tried horse and sheep breeding. Although Brown struggled to pay off his creditors, he kept going deeper into debt. In September 1842, he declared bankruptcy. A court wiped out all his debts but creditors took almost all his possessions except a few items that Brown and his family needed to live. The children, now numbering 12, were crammed into five beds. His family barely had enough to survive.

Things would get worse. In 1843, four of Brown's children died suddenly of an infection of the digestive system known as dysentery. One of Brown's sons would later say that these deaths were "a calamity from which my father never fully recovered." Brown wrote his eldest son: "God has seen fit to visit us with the pestilence and four of our number sleep in the dust. . . . This has been to us all a bitter cup indeed, and we have drunk deeply, but still the Lord reigneth and blessed be his great and holy name forever."

Brown's bankruptcy capped years of poor decision making. He had not been dishonest, but shortsighted and confused. Even by the disorderly investing standards of the day, Brown was more reckless and incompetent in business matters than the average person.

THE WOOL COMMISSION

Finally, things began to look better in 1844, when Brown entered into a partnership with Simon Perkins Jr., a wealthy Akron resident who needed someone to manage his flocks and farms. He agreed to hire Brown and his sons to do it. As usual, Brown threw himself into his work with a passion. He quickly gained the respect of local farmers for his knowledge of various breeds of sheep and types of wool. Brown wrote articles on sheep and wool for local newspapers and agricultural journals. Between 1845 and 1848, 14 articles in the *Ohio Cultivator* contained admiring descriptions of John Brown's work. He began to travel widely as an agent for Perkins's company.

In 1846, Brown convinced Perkins to supply the money to establish a wool commission operation in Springfield, Massachusetts. According to the plan, Brown would run a warehouse in Springfield, where he would store the wool produced in Ohio, Pennsylvania, New York, and Vermont. Brown would price the wool according to its quality, then arrange its sale to companies with the sale price based on the wool's grade. According to Brown, this idea would ensure that the producers of the wool (who owned the sheep) would finally receive a fair price from the New England manufacturers.

Brown possessed an amazing ability for hard work. In Springfield, he labored from daybreak to dusk in the warehouse. He probably sorted and graded about 500,000 pounds of wool in 1847 alone. Yet, despite his energy and enthusiasm, Brown lacked business sense. Completely ignoring supply and demand, he would set what he considered to be a fair price and stubbornly stick to it. He usually overpriced his finest wools while pricing the poorest ones too low. Brown also did not count on the hostility of the mill owners who worked just as hard to ruin his project. He soon found he could not sell the wool that was piling up in the Springfield warehouse.

Brown decided that if he could not dispose of wool in the United States, perhaps he could sell it abroad. He shipped 10 tons of supposedly high-quality wool to Europe and traveled to England seeking a higher price. The trip turned out to be a disaster. Brown had just as much trouble selling the wool, and the company lost almost $40,000. The Perkins and Brown wool commission operation closed in 1849, but the lawsuits lasted for several more years. Brown spent a good deal of 1851 and 1852 in courts, rushing from trial to trial in Pittsburgh, Troy (Ohio), Boston, New York City, and other cities.

Once again, Brown's risk taking revealed bad judgment. His business ideas might make sense, but the actual plans were not well thought out and his expectations were too high. Fortunately for Brown, Perkins absorbed most of the financial losses. Amazingly, although Perkins lost a lot of money, the two men remained friends. Instead of being bitter, he remained mesmerized by Brown's character and convinced of his honesty, if not his business ability.

Brown's business disappointments affected his self-image. He knew that his friends, as well as his enemies, regarded him as a failure. Despite this, John Brown had never completely accepted the American idea that a person's bank account was the measure of his or her value. Throughout these years that he dreamed of riches, he expressed distrust of pursuing wealth too enthusiastically. He wrote, "I trust that getting or losing money does not entirely engross our attention; but I am sensible that it occupies quite too large a share in it." He never completely gave up the hope of making money, but he was looking for some greater purpose or meaning in life. Now over 50, he felt "considerable regret by turns that I have lived so many years, and have in reality done so very little to increase the amount of human happiness." He would find that sense of purpose in his antislavery work.

The Abolitionist

By 1820, there were 1.5 million slaves in the United States and another 200,000 free blacks who suffered tremendous prejudice from whites. Yet, organized opposition to slavery was limited to small groups of free blacks and Quakers. In addition, the American Colonization Society worked to free slaves and send them back to Africa.

The situation changed in 1831, when William Lloyd Garrison began publishing his newspaper, *The Liberator*. Garrison thundered that slavery was a national sin, and he demanded immediate emancipation of the slaves. "I am in earnest," he said in *The Liberator*'s first issue, and "I will not equivocate—I will not excuse—I will not retreat a single inch—AND I WILL BE HEARD!" Brown probably first read *The Liberator* at his father's house during a visit in 1833 or 1834. He soon subscribed to the paper himself.

The American Anti-slavery Society (AASS) was founded in 1833 by abolitionists William Lloyd Garrison, Lewis Tappan, and Arthur Tappan. By 1838, it had 1,350 chapters and 250,000 members. Famous members included Lucretia Mott *(sitting, second from right)*, Frederick Douglass, and Lydia Maria Child.

Garrison was a Christian perfectionist who believed in nonviolence. He thought that abolitionists could simply persuade slave owners to give up their human property. In 1833, Garrison joined forces with Arthur and Lewis Tappan to create the American Anti-slavery Society (AASS). Through their actions, speeches, literature, sermons, and petition drives, the AASS changed slavery from a relative nonissue into the most important moral crusade in American history.

Many women, both white and black, played a key role in the antislavery movement. Lucretia Mott, Lydia Maria Child, and Abigail Kelly Foster all took on an active role in the AASS. Women's names represented more than half the signatures on AASS petitions. Women raised money for the AASS, supported abolitionist speakers, and distributed literature.

The rise of abolitionism often resulted in violent responses from proslavery forces. Riots against abolitionists occurred primarily in Southern states but also in the North in cities such as New York City, Philadelphia, and Utica, New York. In 1835, an anti-abolitionist mob dragged Garrison through the streets of Boston with a rope around his neck, yelling, "Lynch him."

"I CONSECRATE MY LIFE TO THE DESTRUCTION OF SLAVERY"

John Brown's antislavery passion developed at a younger age than most other famous abolitionists. Even as a child, he hated slavery, empathized with the slave, and wanted to change the status quo. Between 1820 and 1840, Brown helped fugitive slaves escape. Hudson, Ohio, was a station on the Underground Railroad. The Underground Railroad was a secret network of routes that made it easier for fugitive slaves to flee to Canada. One of Brown's Ohio neighbors noted that John Brown "considered it as much a duty to help a Negro make his escape as it was to catch a horse thief."

In the mid-1830s, Brown began considering various ideas to help runaway slaves. He talked about adopting black children or building a school for free African Americans. One summer evening in 1836, Brown caused a stir in the Franklin Congregational Church. He insisted that local African Americans join him in his pew instead of sitting in segregated seating at the rear of the church. This shocked even the antislavery members of the church. Like many Northerners, they opposed slavery but did not like black people or support integration.

In 1837, a proslavery mob murdered abolitionist Elijah Lovejoy in Illinois. At a memorial service for Lovejoy, John Brown publicly made an antislavery vow. According to one version of the story, Brown said, "Here, before God, in the presence of these witnesses, from this time, I consecrate my life to the destruction of slavery!"

SPRINGFIELD, MASSACHUSETTS

Between 1838 and 1848, Brown worked as a buyer, seller, and driver of cattle and sheep or as a dealer in wool. His travels brought him into contact with other abolitionists and gave Brown the opportunity to build alliances and assist runaway slaves. In 1846, Brown moved to Springfield, a town of 11,000 in western Massachusetts. For the first time, Brown lived among large numbers of black men and women. Brown quickly won their trust. Blacks were impressed with him and thought his contempt for slave owners seemed nearly as great as their own.

In Springfield, Brown first met Frederick Douglass. Douglass had escaped slavery in Maryland and was a rising star in the abolitionist movement. Douglass had just moved to Rochester, New York, and began publishing an abolitionist newspaper called the *North Star*.

Douglass probably began his long friendship with Brown in late 1847. Douglass visited Brown's home and noted that it had "no sofas, no cushions, no curtains, no carpets, no easy rocking chairs . . . [the home had] an air of plainness about which almost suggested destitution." In fact, it was the best home that Brown had ever inhabited. Douglass wrote in the *North Star*, "The most interesting part of my visit to Springfield, was a private interview with Mr. Brown . . . though a white gentleman, [he] is in sympathy, and is as deeply interested in our cause, as though his own soul had been pierced with the iron of slavery."

That same year, Brown wrote a satirical essay called "Sambo's Mistakes." It was published in *The Ram's Horn*, an abolitionist newspaper published by African Americans in New York City. In this article, Brown pretended to be a free black named Sambo who records all his errors in life in the hope that his fellow blacks will learn from them. Sambo complained that black people had always sought the favor of white men "by tamely submitting to every species of indignity, contempt, and wrong instead of nobly resisting their brutal aggressions from principle. . . ." In his essay, Brown assumed that African Americans were fully capable of improving themselves and assuming their role as citizens of the United States.

While in Springfield, Brown first began to think about what he could do to hamper slavery's progress. Brown thought he could move fugitive slaves to the North through a passage in the Allegheny Mountains modeled after the Underground Railroad. Called the Subterranean Pass Way, Brown's scheme never got beyond the planning stage; however, for the next 10 years Brown continued to think about trying to end slavery.

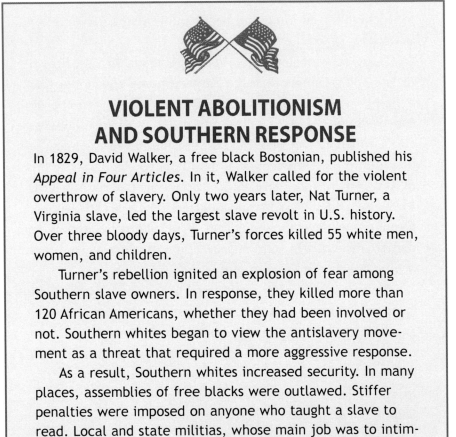

VIOLENT ABOLITIONISM AND SOUTHERN RESPONSE

In 1829, David Walker, a free black Bostonian, published his *Appeal in Four Articles*. In it, Walker called for the violent overthrow of slavery. Only two years later, Nat Turner, a Virginia slave, led the largest slave revolt in U.S. history. Over three bloody days, Turner's forces killed 55 white men, women, and children.

Turner's rebellion ignited an explosion of fear among Southern slave owners. In response, they killed more than 120 African Americans, whether they had been involved or not. Southern whites began to view the antislavery movement as a threat that required a more aggressive response.

As a result, Southern whites increased security. In many places, assemblies of free blacks were outlawed. Stiffer penalties were imposed on anyone who taught a slave to read. Local and state militias, whose main job was to intimidate slaves, increased in size. By 1831, Virginia's security

TIMBUCTOO

In 1846, Gerrit Smith, a wealthy New York land speculator and abolitionist, donated 120,000 acres of land in Essex and Franklin counties in New York to African Americans. Over the next seven years, Smith gave away vast tracts of Adirondack wilderness with the support of Frederick Douglass and other leading black reformers. About 3,000 black New Yorkers received parcels of land.

After Brown's business failures, he decided to move to upstate New York. He thought he could help African Americans establish a community by surveying their properties and advising them in farming methods. In April 1848, Brown met with

force numbered more than 100,000 men, nearly 10 percent of the state's population.

At the same time, Southern whites began to view slavery not as a necessary evil, but now as a positive good. Southern whites claimed that it was better to be a slave on an Alabama cotton plantation than to be free in Africa, or a factory worker in New England. One Southerner wrote, "To attempt to elevate the Negro to the white man's level, is an insult to manhood, a crime against society, and a sin against God."

Slavery proponents also began to use the Bible to support their viewpoint. They pointed out that Jesus never spoke out against slavery. A famous passage from the Bible told slaves to "be obedient to those who are your earthly masters, with fear and trembling." Southern whites preached that slaves could look forward to freedom in the next world (heaven). In the meantime, they should follow the example of Jesus, who died on the cross and suffered in silence rather than using force to fight back.

Smith and told him, "I am something of a pioneer. I will take one of your farms myself, clear it up and plant it, and show my colored neighbors how much work should be done; will give them work as I have occasion, look after them in all needful ways, and be a kind father to them."

Smith liked Brown and sold him 244 acres for a dollar an acre, in the isolated village of North Elba. Brown's farm was located deep in the Adirondacks, far beyond any train line, near Lake Placid. Brown loved his life in the wilds of upstate New York. "I like to live in a country," he said, where "every thing you see reminds one of Omnipotence, and where if you do get your crops cut off once in a while, you will feel your dependence." Brown felt at home in these mountains.

Brown hoped North Elba would develop into a model black community. "There are a number of good colored families on the ground; most of whom I visited," Brown wrote his father. "I can think of no place where I think I would sooner go; all things considered than to live with these poor despised Africans to try, and encourage them; and to show them a little so far as I am capable how to manage."

The various black settlements in the area were known as Timbuctoo after the famous West African city. The guide and farmer Lyman Epps was probably the best known of Timbuctoo's black settlers. Epps quickly became a good friend of Brown's. His son recalled that John Brown would "walk up to our house . . . and come in and play with us children and talk to father. Many's the time I've sat on John Brown's knee. He was a kind and friendly man with children."

Later, Brown discovered that Smith's dream of a community of self-sufficient black farmers was not working. Of the many blacks who received parcels, probably no more than 200 actually moved to the Adirondacks. Brown inspected the scattered farms and noted that the black farmers were having a hard time. Winters were long and bitterly cold. The land was difficult to cultivate and start-up costs for farming were large.

Nobody had surveyed the area, so a person could not be sure if he or she was farming the correct piece of land. Some local whites attempted to cheat the new settlers.

AN INDEPENDENT ABOLITIONIST

Abolitionism was never a popular cause. Out of a U.S. population of 20 million in 1860, only about 20,000 (or 1 percent) of all Americans were abolitionists. Because most people did not support emancipation, abolitionists usually stuck together. They joined antislavery societies and participated in petition drives, sewing circles, and prayer groups.

John Brown was different. Throughout his life, Brown worked outside of organized resistance and reform movements. He never joined any antislavery society or abolitionist group because he had difficulties taking orders from anyone. He was always convinced he was right and therefore unwilling to compromise. A longtime friend and business associate said Brown, "always acted upon his own impulses—he would not listen to anybody."

Brown had, in his son's words, "a cranky sort of piety." Brown read the Bible constantly and believed that each person had to interpret the Bible to the best of his or her individual ability. In the 1840s, he withdrew his membership from the Congregational Church and never officially joined another church.

Brown's radical ideas about racial equality even set him apart from mainstream abolitionists. Unlike most white Americans in the early nineteenth century, he developed personal relationships with black people that were close, trusting, and egalitarian. His family followed his lead.

In June 1849, Brown returned to his cabin in North Elba to find three sunburned, mosquito-bitten men relaxing in the grass. One of them was Richard Henry Dana, a leading Boston attorney. Dana was also the author of the American bestseller, *Two Years before the Mast*, which described Dana's travels as a common seaman. Dana and his friends had come to the

Adirondacks to hunt and fish, but his party had gotten completely lost. They wandered around for 24 hours without food or water before they stumbled onto Brown's single-story log house. He "received us with kindness," Dana later wrote, and invited the men to stay for supper.

Dana had helped found the Free-Soil Party, dedicated to keeping slavery from expanding into the West. Five years later, he would unsuccessfully defend Anthony Burns in Boston against the Fugitive Slave Act. Despite his antislavery credentials, however, the democracy of Brown's family dinner table made Dana uncomfortable. Dana wrote that he and his friends joined "Mr. and Mrs. Brown, and their large family of children, with the hired men and women, including three Negroes, all at the table together." Dana was even more astounded because Brown addressed the black diners politely as if they were his social equals. He introduced the black adults using "Mr." and "Mrs." before their last names. At John Brown's table, blacks were treated as human beings, neither superior nor inferior to whites because of their skin color.

THE FUGITIVE SLAVE ACT OF 1850

After the Mexican-American War of 1846–1848, the United States gained control of Texas and the territory that would later become California, New Mexico, Nevada, Utah, and parts of Colorado, Arizona, and New Mexico. This enormous new territory had been closed to slavery under Mexican law. Whether the U.S. Congress would allow slavery in these new territories became a major political issue in the 1850s.

In 1849, there were 15 slave states and 15 free states. Slaveholders were upset when California applied for admission to the United States as a free state. If California were to gain admission as a free state, the states where slavery was illegal would outnumber the slave states.

Free-Soilers insisted that the national government should make slavery illegal in all the territories taken from Mexico.

The Free-Soil Party had few objections to slavery where it already existed, but they did not want to see it spread. On the other hand, white Southerners said they would support California's admission as a free state only if the U.S. government guaranteed that slavery would always be legal in the United States. Debate in Congress was very bitter and a civil war threatened to break out.

A major crisis was avoided when both sides agreed to a deal called the Compromise of 1850. This series of bills encompassed five laws that balanced the interests of slaves states in the South and free states in the North. California was admitted as a free state. In exchange, Northerners agreed to support the Fugitive Slave Act. This law required that all U.S. citizens participate in the pursuit, recapture, and return of runaway slaves to their owners. Also, Texas received financial compensation for land that was relinquished during the Mexican-American War; the Territory of New Mexico (which included present-day Arizona and a portion of Colorado, Nevada, and New Mexico) was organized without any specific prohibition of slavery; and the slave trade was abolished in the District of Columbia.

The Compromise of 1850 outraged antislavery groups. The law denied a suspected fugitive's right to a jury trial. Instead, special commissioners would handle the cases. The accused fugitive had no right to a lawyer, no right to present evidence, and no right to cross-examine witnesses. A commissioner received $5 if he released the alleged fugitive but $10 if he returned the suspect to slavery. This resulted in the return of 332 suspected fugitives to the South, but only 11 slaves were freed under the Fugitive Slave Act.

Even people across the North who cared nothing about the issue of slavery felt threatened by the increasing power of the slaveholding class in the South. Many Northern states passed "personal liberty laws," providing lawyers for accused fugitives and requiring a trial by jury. Many blacks and whites called for violent resistance to the law. There were several anti-Fugitive

Holy Bible
Thou shalt not deliver unto the master his servant which has escaped from his master unto thee. He shall dwell with thee. Even among you in that place which he shall choose in one of thy gates where it liketh him best. Thou shalt not oppress him.
Deut XXIII.XX.

Effects of the Fugitive-Slave-Law.

Declaration of independence
We hold that all men are created equal, that they are endowed by their Creator with certain unalienable rights, that among these are life, liberty and the pursuit of happiness.

Entered according to Act of Congress in the year 1851 by Hoff & Bloede in the Clerks Office of the District Court of the Southern District of New York.

Effects of the Fugitive Slave Law (above) was made in reaction to the Fugitive Slave Act of 1850. In this print, four black men, possibly freedmen, are ambushed by an armed gang of six white men in a field. Two of the black men have been hit by musket fire as the other two react in shock. Below the picture is text from the book of Deuteronomy in the Bible, which talks about non-oppression, and the other text is from the Declaration of Independence, which declares that all men are created equal.

Slave Law riots in which Northern mobs rescued supposed fugitives and sent them to Canada. Brown wrote his wife, "It now seems that the fugitive slave law was to be the means of making more abolitionists than all the lectures we have had for years."

THE UNITED STATES LEAGUE OF GILEADITES

As a result of the Fugitive Slave Act, Brown formed an all-black resistance organization in Springfield called the United States League of Gileadites (a Biblical reference). Forty-four African-American men and women agreed to join Brown's League of Gileadites. Brown believed whites would respect blacks only when they fought for their independence, just as the British had only begun to respect the Americans after they rebelled. The Gileadites pledged to arm themselves, be ready to use their weapons at all times, and shoot to kill. "Stand by one another and by your friends, while a drop of blood remains," Brown told the group. "Be hanged, if you must, but tell no tales out of school. Make no confessions. Union is strength."

This would not be the last time Brown appealed to African Americans to violently resist slavery. Brown became particularly fond of quoting Hebrews 9:22, which states, "Almost all things are by the law purged with blood; and without the shedding of blood, there is no remission of sin."

Bleeding Kansas

After the Compromise of 1850, the U.S. government opened the territories of Kansas and Nebraska to settlement. "Kansas Fever" swept the country; 126,000 square miles of land west of the Missouri River were now opened to settlement. But would slavery be allowed in these new territories?

The Kansas-Nebraska Act, signed into law in May 1854, placed the explosive issue of slavery into the hands of the people settling the new territories. These people would now decide, by popular vote, whether Kansas and Nebraska should be free or slave states. The act invalidated the Missouri Compromise, which, since 1820, had restricted the expansion of slavery into the West.

The Kansas-Nebraska Act outraged most people in the North. Brown wrote a public letter, published by Frederick

VOTING IN KICKAPOO.

The Kansas-Nebraska Act of 1854 created the territories of Kansas and Nebraska and then let the settlers decide whether to allow slavery within their boundaries. Stephen A. Douglas, who introduced the act, hoped that tensions would be eased between North and South. Instead, both proslavery settlers and abolitionists moved to Kansas for the sole purpose of voting in territorial elections in hopes of influencing whether Kansas would become a free state.

Douglass in the *North Star*, denouncing the U.S. government as "fiends in human shape" who pass "abominably wicked and unjust laws." Opponents of slavery thought the Kansas-Nebraska Act represented another aggressive action by the "slave power conspiracy." Gerrit Smith was elected to Congress in 1852, but he resigned before his term was over. He told Frederick Douglass, "I went to Congress with very little hope of the peaceful termination of American slavery. I have returned with less."

Meanwhile, Missouri's planters and politicians were intent on establishing slavery in Kansas. Thousands of proslavery settlers from Missouri crossed the border. In response, anti-slavery supporters formed the New England Emigrant Aid Company, which sent settlers to Kansas to secure it as a free state. In March 1855, Kansas held an election to choose a territorial legislature. Almost 5,000 men from Missouri, known as "border ruffians," illegally rode into the territory and seized the polling places. Although the Kansas territory had only 2,905 registered voters, more than 6,300 ballots were cast and 87 percent favored slavery. The new territorial legislature passed laws making it illegal to question the fairness of the election or to speak or write against slavery. Helping a fugitive slave could draw the death penalty.

Yet by the fall of 1855, Free-Soil settlers outnumbered pro-slavery people in Kansas. Free-Soilers refused to follow the laws made by the fraudulent legislature. Instead, they organized a convention in October 1855 and elected a free state constitu-tion. In 1856, Kansas had two governments: an official proslav-ery one at Lecompton and a Free-Soil government at Topeka that represented the majority of settlers.

THE BROWNS MOVE TO KANSAS

In mid-1855, John Brown's adult sons—Owen, Salmon, John Jr., Jason, and Frederick—and their families joined the thousands of Northern settlers moving to Kansas. The territory had better soil and a more temperate climate than New York. However, Brown's sons also went to keep Kansas free of slavery.

Brown decided not to go. He was 55, almost an old man by the standards of the time. "If you or any of my family are

THE CANING OF SENATOR SUMNER

Southern society could be particularly violent. Whipping, tarring and feathering, stabbing, hanging, and even torture were common features of not only master/slave relations but also white-on-white relations. Southern whites often attacked each other in the name of honor. Massachusetts senator Charles Sumner learned this first-hand on May 22, 1856.

On May 19 and 20, Sumner delivered a speech entitled, "The Crime Against Kansas." The speech attacked President Franklin Pierce and Southerners who sympathized with pro-slavery violence in Kansas. In particular, Sumner criticized South Carolina senator Andrew Butler, who was not present when Sumner read the speech. Butler's nephew, South Carolina representative Preston Brooks, wanted revenge. Brooks decided that Sumner was not his social equal and therefore a duel would be inappropriate. Instead, Brooks decided the honorable thing to do was to attack Sumner from behind with a cane.

Two days after the speech, Brooks found Sumner writing at his desk in the U.S. Senate chamber. Brooks said, "Mr. Sumner, I have read your speech twice over carefully. It is a libel on South Carolina, and Mr. Butler, who is a relative of mine." As Sumner began to stand up, Brooks began beating Sumner on the head with his thick wooden cane. Sumner became caught under the heavy desk that was bolted to the floor. Yet Brooks continued to bash Sumner until the desperate man ripped the desk from the floor. Sumner, blinded by his own blood, collapsed unconscious on the floor. Brooks continued to beat Sumner until he finally broke his cane. Then he walked out of the Senate.

(continues)

(continued)

Sumner was so badly injured he did not return to the Senate for three years. Yet most white Southerners considered Brooks a hero for beating his defenseless opponent. The House of Representatives could not even get the votes to expel Brooks from Congress. Brooks resigned anyway, but South Carolinians admired him so much that they quickly reelected him. The *Richmond Enquirer* crowed, "We consider the act good in conception, better in execution, and best of all in consequences. These vulgar abolitionists in the Senate . . . must be lashed into submission."

In the North, however, Brooks's unannounced attack was regarded as the act of a violent and cowardly barbarian. Brown's son Jason remembered that when his father and brothers heard the news, "the men went crazy—crazy. It seemed to be the finishing, decisive touch." When someone advised Brown to use caution, he replied, "Caution, caution, sir. I am eternally tired of hearing that word caution. It is nothing but the word of cowardice."

disposed to go to Kansas or Nebraska," he wrote John Jr., "with a view to help defeat Satan and his legions in that direction, I have not a word to say; but I feel committed to operate in another part of the field."

Letters from his sons in Kansas changed Brown's mind. They wrote that proslavery forces were preparing to attack Free Soilers and their families. His sons described thousands of men, armed to the teeth, thoroughly organized, and in the pay of slaveholders. Against these stood the friends of freedom, "not one fourth of them half-armed." The Free-Soilers needed high quality weapons, such as large Colt revolvers and rapid-fire Sharps rifles.

Brown was energized. He was determined to protect his family and oppose the advances of proslavery supporters. In June 1855, he packed a wagon and headed west, gathering weapons and funds along the way. He did not have a definite plan. One of his daughters later said that, "Father said his object in going to Kansas was to see if something would not turn up to his advantage."

THE SACK OF LAWRENCE

When Brown arrived at his sons' homestead in Kansas, he found them shivering with fever in makeshift tents. They were too weak to work and almost starving to death. John Brown wrote his own father, "I felt very much disappointed at finding all my children here in such very uncomfortable circumstances." In three weeks, Brown built a sturdy log cabin and quickly brought order to their homestead, known as "Brown's Station." Brown never owned property or built a house for himself in Kansas. He sometimes stayed with his half sister Florella and brother-in-law, Samuel Adair, at their cabin in Osawatomie.

John Jr. was the captain of the Pottawatomie Rifles, a small group of free-state men living near Pottawatomie Creek. They frequently exchanged threats of violence with their proslavery neighbors but an uneasy truce reigned. Most of the Northerners in Kansas resented being called abolitionists. These Free-Soilers disliked blacks and hoped to keep them out of Kansas. They wanted to make the territory free of slavery, but free and white. They objected to slavery mainly because they felt poor whites could not compete against slave labor.

In November 1855, an army of Missourians crossed the state line and began a siege of the free state town of Lawrence. Brown loaded a wagon with food and weapons and set out for Lawrence. In town, he was quickly commissioned captain in the 1st Brigade of Kansas Volunteers and given command of a small company of men. Although the situation did not come to violence, Brown now had a new identity. He was a man of action, a fighter who would stand up to slaveholders and their allies.

Through most of the winter of 1855–1856, men and women worried more about the bitter cold than slavery. "Thermometer on Sunday and Monday at 28 to 29 below zero . . ." Brown wrote his wife. "Oliver was laid up by freezing his toes. . . . He will be crippled for some days yet. Owen has one foot some frozen. . . . All mail communications are entirely cut off by the snowdrifts." Yet the Browns kept hearing stories of Southern aggression in Kansas. President Franklin Pierce, a New Hampshire man sympathetic to slavery, firmly backed the fraudulent legislature. Brown believed a vast slave-power conspiracy was working to spread slavery into Kansas and across the United States.

On May 21, 1856, an army of Missourians sacked the free state town of Lawrence. The ruffians decimated the newspaper offices, burned and looted homes, and destroyed the Free State Hotel. They caused more than $200,000 worth of damage.

The Browns and their allies quickly assembled to help the people of Lawrence. On the way, they received another disturbing report. Massachusetts senator Charles Sumner had been brutally attacked and almost beaten to death in the U.S. Senate by a Southern member of the House of Representatives. One Kansas newspaper wrote that proslavery forces were determined to "make Kansas a Slave State; though . . . the carcasses of the Abolitionists should be so numerous in the territory as to breed disease and sickness, we will not be deterred from our purpose."

The violence of the proslavery forces outraged Brown. He also resented the cowardly response of the free state settlers. "Something is going to be done now," Brown said. "We must show by actual work that there are two sides to this thing, and that they cannot go on with impunity." Brown believed

Northerners had to stop Southern proslavery aggression, peacefully if possible, but by the use of force if necessary.

BROWN'S CHILDREN

Like his father, John Brown ruled his household with a Bible in one hand and a rod in the other. His oldest son, John Jr., remembered, "Father had a rule not to threaten one of his children. He commanded, and there was obedience." Brown could be harsh with his own children. "The trouble is," John Jr. once said, "you want your boys to be brave as tigers, and still afraid of you."

Brown also had a softer side. He wanted to be both feared and loved. One of his daughters, Ruth, remembered, "He sometimes seemed very stern and strict with me; yet his tenderness made me forget that he was stern." The four daughters who lived to maturity all idolized their father.

Of his sons who lived to adulthood, John Jr. seemed the most like his father. John Jr. was a blunt-talking abolitionist always ready for action. Bright and sensitive, Jason hated violence; he was a quiet, gentle man who had never even had a fistfight. The copper-haired Owen suffered a childhood injury that permanently crippled his left arm. He often quarreled with his father but remained deeply loyal to him. Simple and unstable, Frederick suffered from blinding headaches, fits of delirium, and other strange behaviors that began in his early teens. Tall and athletic, both Watson and Salmon grew to be tough, stubborn, and ferociously opposed to slavery. Oliver was the youngest son of Brown's to reach adulthood. He was physically the strongest and a voracious reader, even more so than his father.

Brown did not force any of his children to become abolitionists. As they got older, they argued with him over religion and tactics. To some degree, they rejected his Calvinist views. Yet, none of Brown's children ever distanced themselves from their father and he never turned away from them. Not one abandoned the cause of abolition and racial equality that Brown championed.

POTTAWATOMIE

After the sack of Lawrence and the caning of Senator Sumner, Brown declared, "Something must be done to show these barbarians that we, too, have rights." He took a small group of men under his command and told them to prepare for a secret mission. John Jr. tried to keep his father in camp, calling out to him, "Father, be careful, and commit no rash act." Nevertheless, the old man was intent on some act of retaliation. Brown and his men marched toward Pottawatomie Creek, to the homes of proslavery sympathizers. Some, he believed, had marked his own family for attack because of their antislavery views. Brown told his men it was time to "fight fire with fire," and to "strike terror in the hearts of the proslavery people."

On the night of May 24, 1856, Brown and six others—his sons Frederick, Salmon, Oliver, and Owen, his son-in-law Henry Thompson, and James Townsley—banged on the door of James Doyle. They announced themselves as the Northern Army and ordered the three Doyle men to come outside. There they attacked them with broadswords, splitting open heads and cutting off arms. This was more of an execution than a war. When they finished the slaughter, Brown put a bullet into the head of James Doyle. Mrs. Doyle later testified that Brown told her, "if a man stood between him and what he considered right, he would take his life as coolly as he would eat his breakfast." Brown's group visited two more cabins on the Pottawatomie. They dragged out and killed two more men in the same brutal fashion, slashing and stabbing them to death.

Although the slaughter at Pottawatomie was considered one of Brown's most controversial acts, his sons later insisted that their father did not go on a random murder spree. Instead, they claimed, he had chosen his targets carefully. The victims were active in proslavery politics, had challenged the Brown family personally, and had been involved in intimidating and threatening free state settlers. Nonetheless, they owned no slaves and committed no crimes to justify their execution.

Outraged by what he thought was a cowardly response to the violence being inflicted on antislavery settlers by proslavery forces, and also learning of a planned attack against his family, John Brown and a group of abolitionist settlers massacred five proslavery settlers in May 1856. This and other bloody episodes preceded the American Civil War.

Proslavery men had murdered six free-state men since the struggle had begun in Kansas. If nothing else, Brown had shown that free staters were also capable of violence. In murdering five proslavery men, Brown and his Northern Army tried to even the score.

Whether John Brown participated directly in the killings has long been a matter of dispute. Nonetheless, he was the leader of the expedition and, in the end, responsible for its results. Surviving accounts seem to imply that Salmon and Owen performed the bloody deeds in front of their father. When confronted by Jason, his son with nonviolent tendencies, Brown said, "I did not do it but I approved it." When Jason replied that he thought it was a wicked act, Brown replied, "God is my judge; and the people will yet justify my course."

As it turned out, God would be the only judge of John Brown for the Pottawatomie killings. A court indicted him for murder, but the case was not heard immediately because of the disorganized state of Kansas's legal system. In the meantime, Brown and his followers hid out in the woods, resurfacing occasionally to battle proslavery forces.

BATTLE OF BLACK JACK

Brown's attack, like most previous killings over the slavery issue in Kansas, went officially unpunished. Unofficially, however, proslavery forces plundered free-state homesteads as they searched for the Pottawatomie killers. Two of Brown's sons—John Jr. and Jason—were savagely beaten and jailed even though they had not been involved at Pottawatomie. Proslavery forces burned Brown's Station to the ground.

Southeastern Kansas was in complete chaos. Dozens of settlers on both sides fled the region in fear for their lives. Wandering bands prowled the countryside, shooting at one another, burning cabins, attacking settlements, stealing horses, and looting enemy stores and homesteads. The sacking of Lawrence and the assassinations at Pottawatomie had triggered a terrible guerrilla war.

At dawn on June 2, 1856, Brown, 9 of his followers, and 20 local men successfully attacked a proslavery militia. The battle took place at a popular camping ground along the Santa Fe Trail near Black Jack Creek. Although Brown's men were outnumbered, they made the Missouri forces surrender after three hours of intense fighting. The Free Staters captured 22 men in addition to horses and military stores. Brown was very proud of his victory over the Missourians. He wrote his wife that Black Jack was the "first regular battle fought between Free State and proslavery men in Kansas."

Brown's victory at Black Jack made headlines across the United States. Liking the interest in his story and the publicity, Brown began to work hard to gain the friendship and support of journalists such as James Redpath, Richard Hinton, and especially William Addison Phillips. Phillips later wrote that Brown was "always an enigma, a strange compound of enthusiasm and cold, methodic stolidity—a volcano beneath a mountain of snow."

OSAWATOMIE

In August 1856, a company of 300 Missourians again crossed into Kansas. These border ruffians intended to destroy the free state settlements at Osawatomie and then march on Topeka and Lawrence. On the morning of August 30, they shot and killed Brown's son Frederick and his neighbor David Garrison on the outskirts of Pottawatomie.

Brown decided to try to stop them from committing further havoc. Outnumbered more than seven to one, Brown arranged his 38 men behind natural defenses along the road near Osawatomie. Firing from cover, they killed about 20 of the proslavery raiders and wounded 40 more. Eventually, Brown's small group scattered and fled across the Marais des Cygnes River. One of Brown's men was killed during the retreat and four were captured. While Brown and his surviving men hid in the nearby woods, the Missourians burned Osawatomie. Brown was incensed. "I have only a short time to live—only one death to die," he said, "and I will die fighting for this cause. There will be no more peace in this land until slavery is done for."

Despite the defeat, Brown's bravery and military shrewdness in the face of long odds at Osawatomie brought him more national attention. William Addison Phillips described Brown as "a strange, resolute, repulsive, iron-willed, inexorable old man." Brown became a hero to many Northern abolitionists. John Jr., who was still in prison, wrote his father that the "Battle of Osawatomie is considered here as the great fight so far. . . . This has proved most unmistakably that 'Yankees' WILL 'fight.' Everyone I hear speaking of you is loud in your praise. The Missourians in this region show signs of great fear."

A LULL IN THE ACTION

On September 7, 1856, Brown entered Lawrence to help defend the town against an assault by several thousand proslavery Missourians. Before a major battle could occur, Kansas Territorial governor John Geary intervened to prevent any violence. Geary was a 6-foot, 5-inch native Pennsylvanian who fought in the Mexican War and took no nonsense from anyone. In time, Geary brought peace to Kansas and ended the fighting that took almost 200 lives and cost nearly $2 million.

Brown took advantage of the fragile peace to leave Kansas with three of his sons. He wanted to raise money from supporters in the North. On his way east, Brown stopped in Ohio to visit his half brother Jeremiah. Jeremiah noted a marked change in his brother. Jeremiah wrote, "Previous to this, he [John Brown] devoted himself entirely to business; but since these troubles he has abandoned all business, and has become wholly absorbed by the subject of slavery. . . . I urged him to go home . . . that I feared his course would prove his destruction and that of the boys. . . . He replied that . . . he knew that he was in the line of his duty, and he must pursue it, though it should destroy him and his family."

Pottawatomie, Black Jack, and Osawatomie changed the equation in Kansas. Before Brown's actions, Southerners viewed abolitionists as laughable cowards who were afraid to fight (such as at the sack of Lawrence) or could not fight (such as Charles Sumner). After Pottawatomie, however, Southerners described abolitionists as ferocious criminals intent on attacking Southern institutions. One person said, "There is no one whom the ruffians entertain a more wholesome dread than Captain Brown. They hate him as they would a snake, but their hatred is composed nine-tenths of fear." Brown frightened the South because he was an abolitionist who was committed to armed warfare against slavery and showed no signs of relenting.

A War
Against Slavery

By November 1856, Brown had returned to the East to raise money. He had changed greatly from the man who had gone to Kansas a year before. The failed businessperson was now a national celebrity. He was "Old Brown" now, or "Osawatomie Brown," the terror of proslavery forces in Kansas. Brown's successes inspired him to develop new ideas for future assaults against slavery.

In January 1857, Brown went to the Massachusetts State Kansas Committee (a group that raised $100,000 in money and supplies throughout Massachusetts, which they sent to the Kansas people) searching for money, supplies, and guns to continue his fight against proslavery forces. Brown met with Franklin Sanborn, the 26-year-old idealist who served as the committee's secretary. Brown entertained Sanborn with stories of bloody fighting in Kansas. By the end of their meeting, Sanborn agreed to help Brown as much as possible. In a March lecture, Sanborn told a Concord, Massachusetts, audience, "If this nation was to have a war over slavery, then the forces of freedom would need men like John Brown."

Brown raised money for the fight against proslavery forces by giving lectures throughout New England and New York. Sanborn introduced Brown to influential abolitionists in the Boston area. Early in 1857, Brown met William Lloyd Garrison for the only time. They had a friendly disagreement; each time Garrison referred to the pacifism of Jesus, Brown countered with the bloody prophecies of Jeremiah. Sanborn also introduced Brown to his Concord friends, the writers Henry David Thoreau and Ralph Waldo Emerson. Brown impressed both men and they contributed small amounts of money to his cause. His adventures in Kansas had appeared widely in many Northern newspapers. Brown's fund-raising appearances stirred excitement. Abolitionists were proud to meet a true freedom fighter from bleeding Kansas. To them, Brown seemed like a hero straight out of the pages of a romantic novel.

Brown hoped to raise $30,000. He received many pledges but little cash. Brown grew discouraged with fund-raising. "I am literally driven to beg," he said, "which is very humiliating."

THE SECRET SIX

A group of six wealthy radical abolitionists—Thomas Wentworth Higginson, Theodore Parker, George Luther Stearns,

(*Opposite page*) A month after the start of the American Civil War, "John Brown's Song" was played for the first time. Later, newspapers reported Union soldiers singing the song as they marched through the streets of Boston, and it became a popular marching song during the American Civil War. The lyrics, which praised John Brown, were later changed to the legendary "Battle Hymn of the Republic."

John Brown's
ORIGINAL
Marching Song.

TUNE.—Brothers, will you meet me.

John Brown's body lies a-mouldering in the grave;
John Brown's body lies a-mouldering in the grave;
John Brown's body lies a-mouldering in the grave;
    His soul's marching on!

CHORUS.
Glory, halle—hallelujah!   Glory, halle—hallelujah!
Glory, halle—hallelujah! his soul's marching on!

He's gone to be a soldier in the army of the Lord!
He's gone to be a soldier in the army of the Lord!
He's gone to be a soldier in the army of the Lord!
    His soul's marching on!

John Brown's knapsack is strapped upon his back!
John Brown's knapsack is strapped upon his back!
John Brown's knapsack is strapped upon his back!
    His soul's marching on!

His pet lambs will meet him on the way;
His pet lambs will meet him on the way;
His pet lambs will meet him on the way;
    They go marching on!

They will hang Jeff. Davis to a tree!
They will hang Jeff. Davis to a tree!
They will hang Jeff. Davis to a tree!
    As they march along!

Now, three rousing cheers for the Union;
Now, three rousing cheers for the Union;
Now, three rousing cheers for the Union;
    As we are marching on!

Johnson, Song Publisher, Stationer & Printer, No. 7
N. Tenth St., 3 doors above Market, Phila.

See Johnson's New Catalogue of Songs.

Samuel Gridley Howe, Franklin Sanborn, and Gerrit Smith—agreed to secretly finance Brown's antislavery activities. They represented a cross section of upperclass Northern society: two ministers, a physician, an industrialist, an educator, and a philanthropist. They became known as the Secret Six.

Thomas Wentworth Higginson was both a minister and an amateur boxer. He was descended from one of the oldest European families in New England. He was a romantic who would later lead the first black regiment in the Civil War, write a wide range of books, and help popularize the work of Emily Dickinson.

Samuel Gridley Howe pioneered important educational reforms for the blind, deaf, and feebleminded. He was also a dashing adventurer who had fought in the Greek Revolution for six years against Turkey and aided Polish rebels against Russia. In the United States, he helped dozens of fugitive slaves escape through Boston. His wife, Julia Ward Howe, later wrote the lyrics to "John Brown's Song" known as "The Battle Hymn of the Republic."

George Luther Stearns was a self-made Yankee businessperson. He earned large fortunes as a linseed oil processor and a lead pipe manufacturer. He joined the antislavery movement in the early 1840s. Stearns gave a great deal of money to antislavery homesteaders to help settle Kansas. In the Civil War, he would play a crucial role in enlisting black soldiers for the Union cause.

Many people considered Theodore Parker the greatest American orator of the time. He was a controversial Unitarian minister who rejected all miracles, denied the authority of Jesus, and saw the Bible as full of contradictions and mistakes. However, he retained his faith in a merciful God and an immortal soul. Parker supported several reform movements besides abolition.

Most of the Secret Six were disunionists. They thought the only solution to Southern slave power was to break apart the United States. They generally supported any actions that might bring on a civil war. For this reason, they did not necessarily frown on the use of violence. The Secret Six would eventually provide most of the financial backing for John Brown's raids. Brown often requested help from them. It remains unclear how much each member of the Secret Six knew about any of Brown's schemes.

A NEW PLAN TAKES SHAPE

Brown's experiences in Kansas changed his ideas about how to attack slavery. Previously, he had wanted to encourage slaves to flee to the mountains or to Canada. Now he played with the idea of establishing a free state in the middle of the South. By 1858, Brown no longer looked toward Kansas. Instead, his gaze began to drift to western Virginia.

To his friends, Brown floated the idea of raising an armed band and invading the South somewhere near the Blue Ridge Mountains of Virginia. He thought a small group of well-disciplined raiders could defend the narrow valleys of western Virginia against even the best Southern soldiers. They could fight a guerrilla war that would spread throughout the South. Thousands of slaves would desert their masters and wage war on plantations on both sides of the Appalachians. Free blacks in the North and Canada would rally to the aid of the invaders. Brown's victorious force would set up a new free state in the conquered territory of the South. Once this free state was established, surrounding states would be forced to emancipate their slaves and the institution would collapse.

Guerrilla warfare in the South seemed possible. In 1859–1860, Garibaldi, the Italian revolutionary, conquered Sicily using guerrilla warfare. Fugitive slaves had created successful communities on the island nations of Suriname, Haiti, and most famously, in Jamaica.

Brown's revolutionary scheme, however, would require exceptional leadership, carefully mapped out tactics, and well-planned training. Assuming Brown could actually establish his free state, how could he defend it against the power of Southern slave owners, militias, and the state and federal government? As in his business career, Brown did not trouble himself with details. Brown's confidence stemmed from his belief that he was chosen by God to rid the land of slavery.

ABOLITIONISTS ACCEPT VIOLENCE

In early 1857, James Buchanan was inaugurated president of the United States. One of his first acts was to urge Congress to admit Kansas to the Union as a slave state. Almost immediately afterward, the U.S. Supreme Court ruled in the *Dred Scott* decision that Congress could not declare slavery illegal because a slave was a form of property protected by the Constitution.

To abolitionists, the power of the proslavery forces now seemed almost unstoppable. It was one thing to talk about using democratic means to end slavery, but politics seemed hopelessly stacked against antislavery supporters. The Three-Fifths Compromise (which counted slaves as part of a state's population) had given the South unfair political power. Of the first 15 presidents, 9 owned slaves and 2 (Buchanan and Pierce) were Southern sympathizers. These presidents picked the Supreme Court justices who also usually owned slaves. No constitutional amendment against slavery would ever pass the Senate; an amendment needed a two-thirds vote but Southerners always controlled more than one-third of the Senate. The fact that each state had two senators wiped out the North's population advantage. All three branches of government seemed closed off to antislavery supporters.

Abolitionists felt thoroughly defeated. They could only agree with New York senator William Seward, who had said in 1850, "there is a higher law than the Constitution." Twenty years of preaching about the sins of slavery had not brought emancipation but an increase of almost half a million slaves.

Many black and some white abolitionists had regarded violence as a possible way to end slavery. What did the Declaration of Independence mean if not that an oppressed

THE *DRED SCOTT* DECISION

The *Dred Scott v. Sandford* case, often considered the worst decision ever made by the U.S. Supreme Court, convinced many abolitionists that there was no possible solution to the slavery issue outside of violence.

Dred Scott was a slave whose owner took him to Illinois and Wisconsin, which was then part of the Illinois Territory in the 1830s. Scott and his wife, Harriet, had lived in these places, where slavery was illegal, for two years. In 1846, Scott sued for his freedom in St. Louis, Missouri. He claimed that living in a free territory and/or a free state made him free. Eventually, the case made its way to the U.S. Supreme Court in 1856.

The Supreme Court had to consider three questions:

1. Was Dred Scott a citizen of the United States? That is, did he have legal status to sue in the U.S. Supreme Court?

2. Did residence in a free state and free territory make Dred Scott free?

3. Did the U.S. Congress have the right to prohibit slavery in a territory or even allow a territorial legislature to make this decision?

U.S. Supreme Court justices were chosen by the president and approved by the Senate. In 1857, the nine-member Supreme Court included five Southern judges, all of whom came from slaveholding families. Northern presidents had appointed only two of the justices. On March 6, 1857, the Supreme Court ruled against Scott, finding that:

1. People of African descent, even if they were free, could never be citizens of the United States. The decision

(continues)

(continued)
stated that blacks were "so far inferior, that they had
no rights which a white man was bound to respect."

2. Residence in a free state or territory did not make
   Scott free. Slaves were private property and could not
   be "taken" from their owners without due process.

3. Congress had no authority to prohibit slavery in federal territories. This meant that the Missouri Compromise was unconstitutional.

The *Dred Scott* decision, along with the Kansas-
Nebraska Act, overturned the compromises between
the North and the South that had existed for years. The
actions of the government seemed to confirm every fear
Northerners had about the slave power conspiracy. It
seemed to make it impossible to prohibit slavery anywhere. Abraham Lincoln claimed the next Supreme Court
decision would allow some form of legal Northern slavery.
The *Dred Scott* decision helped radicalize the North and
bring on the Civil War.

people might use force to gain freedom if no other means was
available? Even nonviolent abolitionists admired black libera-
tors such as Haiti's Toussaint Louverture, American rebel Nat
Turner, and West African Joseph Cinque, who led a revolt on
a ship called the *Amistad.*

The Fugitive Slave Act led to violent resistance. Dramatic
rescues of accused fugitive slaves had taken place in Boston,
Massachusetts (1851); Syracuse, New York (1851); Christiana,
Pennsylvania (1852); Boston again (1854); and Oberlin, Ohio
(1858). Abolitionists of both races defied the law. Frederick

James Buchanan, the fifteenth president of the United States, was a "doughface," or a Northerner with Southern sympathies. Buchanan supported slavery, and it was widely believed that he had been personally involved in the outcome of the *Dred Scott* decision. Consistently ranked as one of the worst U.S. presidents, Buchanan is blamed for not taking a harder line against the states that threatened to secede from the Union leading up to the Civil War.

Douglass, who discouraged slave revolts in the 1840s, now supported physical resistance to the Fugitive Slave Act. Abolitionist and women's rights advocate Angelina Grimké

Weld said, "We are compelled to choose between two evils, and all we can do is take the least, and baptize liberty in blood, if it must be so." By the late 1850s, abolitionists such as William Lloyd Garrison, who continued to insist on nonviolence, were in the minority.

Brown believed in the use of violence to free the slaves long before most other white abolitionists. At a convention of the New England Antislavery Society, he grew impatient listening to the long speeches about overthrowing slavery. "Talk! Talk! Talk! That will never free the slaves," he complained. "What is needed is action—action." In March 1857, Brown contracted a Connecticut blacksmith to make 1,000 pikes. These pikes had a two-edged knife on top of a six-foot pole. Brown thought these pikes would be the perfect tool for slaves who did not know how to use guns.

RECRUITING AN ARMY

In the summer of 1857, John Brown went to Tabor, Iowa. He waited there for three months, but violence between Free-Soilers and proslavery forces had almost ceased in Kansas. In October, Kansas free-staters won an overwhelming victory in a fair election. They sent a free-state man to Congress and captured 33 of the 52 seats in the new Kansas legislature. The slavery struggle in Kansas was virtually over. If Brown wanted to fight slavery, it would have to be somewhere else.

In November 1857, Brown persuaded nine antislavery men—one escaped slave and eight white men—to train for a new and secret assignment. Five of these men would remain with Brown over the next two years and go with him to Harpers Ferry, Virginia. They were John Kagi, John Cook, Aaron Stevens, Charles Tidd, and William Leeman.

John Kagi was the intensely idealistic son of an Ohio blacksmith. Kagi came to Kansas in 1855 after losing his job as a schoolteacher in Virginia because of his antislavery views. He met Brown in Lawrence and became one of his closest advisors.

Kagi also served as a reporter for several eastern newspapers in Kansas. He fought with free-state militia units and served four months in jail for his antislavery activities.

John Edwin Cook was the son of a wealthy Connecticut family. He studied for a time at Yale and then worked as a law clerk in Brooklyn before moving to Kansas. He met Brown just before the Battle of Black Jack and served in Brown's militia unit for the rest of the summer of 1856.

Aaron Stevens possessed the most military experience of Brown's recruits. At age 16, Stevens had run away from his Massachusetts home, where his father and older brothers were music teachers. He fought in a volunteer company in the Mexican-American War and enlisted in the U.S. Army in 1851. In 1855, Stevens assaulted an abusive superior officer and received three years of hard labor in Fort Leavenworth, Kansas. Stevens escaped from military prison, changed his name to Charles Whipple, and became a commanding officer of the free-state militia. He met Brown in Kansas in 1856 and became one of his bravest and most devoted followers.

Charles Plummer Tidd was a quick-tempered settler who had come to Kansas from Maine in 1856. He could be sarcastic and loved teasing the other men, but he was a good friend of John Cook's.

William Leeman had worked in a shoe factory in Haverhill, Massachusetts, since the age of 14. He left home in 1855 and arrived in Kansas just in time to fight with Brown at Ossawatomie.

Brown's new recruits assumed that the mission he had in mind was liberating slaves along the Missouri border. They were adventurous men, all in their twenties, except Leeman, who was 18. They detested slavery and wanted to fight it. Still, they were shocked when Brown told them that his goal was not to attack slavery in Kansas but to strike at Virginia. Several of Brown's men, especially Cook, strongly disagreed. The charismatic Brown managed to convince them all.

The group moved its supplies to Springdale, Iowa, an anti-slavery settlement about 50 miles from the Illinois border. This meant traveling 285 miles across Iowa in the middle of winter. Yet they did it cheerfully, all the while engaged in philosophical discussions and arguments at every wintry encampment. At Springdale, the young men rented a farmhouse. They flirted with the Quaker girls and argued about religion and politics. Stevens wrote his sister, "I am ready to give up my life for the oppressed if need be. I hope I shall have your good will and sympathy in this glorious cause."

Brown picked up some additional recruits at Springdale. These included a 22-year-old Canadian by the name of Stewart Taylor and two Ohio-born Quaker brothers—18-year-old Barclay Coppoc and 22-year-old Edwin Coppoc. Although Quakers are usually pacifists, the Coppoc brothers were perfectly willing to take up arms against slavery.

THE PROVISIONAL CONSTITUTION

In January 1858, Brown visited Frederick Douglass in Rochester, New York. Brown stayed at Douglass's house for almost a month. He tried to persuade Douglass to join his planned guerrilla war from a base in the Appalachian Mountains. He talked about it so much that Douglass later wrote, "I confess it began to be something of a bore to me." Douglass did agree to raise money and recruits in black communities in the Northeast. By 1860, more than 125,000 blacks lived in New York, New Jersey, and Pennsylvania, and another 20,000 in New England. Brown hoped to persuade many of them to join his army, or at least to give him material support.

A young black man, Shields Green, was often at Douglass's house. Green, born Esau Brown, had escaped from slavery by boat in South Carolina. In 1858, Green returned to Rochester from Canada and opened a clothes-cleaning business. He was uneducated and rarely spoke, but he had an air of dignity about him. Green took a liking to Brown, who seemed to hate slavery as much as he did. It would not be the last time they would meet.

While Brown was at Douglass's house, he composed a document grandly named "Provisional Constitution and Ordinances for the People of the United States." This amazing document created a government for a new free state in the area of his invasion.

Brown's provisional constitution set up a government with a president, an assembly, and a court system of elected judges. In 48 articles, the provisional constitution covered almost every aspect of daily life. Brown dedicated his document to oppressed African Americans. He declared slavery to be "in utter disregard and violation of those eternal and self-evident truths set forth in our Declaration of Independence." Therefore, all slaveholders' property would be confiscated.

Brown then traveled to upstate New York to discuss matters with Gerrit Smith and Franklin Sanborn. In letters to them, Brown had indicated that he wanted to go into the South to do "Kansas work." Now Brown laid out his entire plan to attack slavery in western Virginia and arm fugitive slaves. "We listened until after midnight, proposing objections and raising difficulties," Sanborn said, "but nothing could shake the purpose of the Old Puritan." Brown told the two men he needed only $800 to make the plan work. When Sanborn protested the "hopelessness of undertaking anything so vast with such slender means," Brown replied, "If God be for us, who can be against us?"

"You see how it is," Smith told Sanborn. "Our dear friend has made up his mind to this course, and cannot be turned from it. We cannot give him up to die alone; we must support him." Sanborn later remembered, "[It was] an amazing proposition—desperate in its character, seemingly inadequate in its provision of means, and of very uncertain results. . . . But . . . he left us only the alternatives of betrayal, desertion, or support. We chose the last."

On the Brink

One of the last stops on the Underground Railroad was Chatham, Ontario, 45 miles east of Detroit. Slavery was illegal in Canada, and about one-third of Chatham's 6,000 residents were fugitive slaves from the United States. The blacks had organized schools, churches, a newspaper, a fire company, and several civic organizations. They were part of the 75,000-strong black community in British Canada.

In May 1858, Brown and 12 of his followers traveled to Chatham. With the help of black activist Martin Delany, they held a secret constitutional convention for the revolutionary state that Brown hoped to create. The convention assembled 34 blacks and 12 whites to hear Brown's plans. Brown was disappointed in the turnout. None of his influential friends and backers had come to Chatham. Still, Brown wanted to go ahead. He hoped to gain support from volunteers in Canada.

Martin Delaney was a physician, writer, newspaper publisher, abolitionist, and strong supporter of black nationalism. Delaney created the *North Star* with Frederick Douglass, and later became the first black field officer in the U.S. Army. Delaney and other prominent blacks who once supported Brown and his cause distanced themselves from Brown as his actions became more militant and unpredictable.

Brown had been clean-shaven all his life, but in the last few months he had let his beard grow. It had come in white, full, and wild. As he rose to address the convention, he seemed to be the living picture of a Bible prophet. To the assembled delegates, Brown laid out his plan to attack slavery by invading the Blue Ridge Mountains in Virginia. He stated that, "for twenty or thirty years the idea had possessed him like a passion of giving liberty to the slaves."

No one at the convention objected to a direct, armed attack on slavery in the South. But how would Brown's forces evade or defeat the militias sent into the mountains to destroy them? And would slaves risk rising up to follow a white man in bearing arms against their masters? Brown had heard both objections before. He argued that a small force could avoid destruction just as in Kansas. Brown was also convinced that Southern slaves were ready to revolt. They just lacked a leader.

The convention then heard John Kagi read Brown's provisional constitution. Only Article 46 drew debate. This article denied any intention to overthrow state or federal governments. It also stated that, "our flag shall be the same that our Fathers fought under in the Revolution." One black delegate noted that slaves had no love for the Stars and Stripes; many of them already carried America's stripes on their backs. Brown urged that the flag remain a symbol of the true meaning of the American republic. The provisional constitution passed unanimously.

Although all of the delegates signed the constitution, few, if any, volunteered to join Brown's forces. Shortly afterward, Brown left Canada and nearly 17 months passed without any action. By the time Brown was ready to move, the ex-slaves of Chatham had lost whatever enthusiasm they had for Brown's plan.

Brown, however, did meet two valuable people in Chatham. Osborne Perry Anderson was a young black printer who moved to Canada in 1850. Born in Pennsylvania, Anderson had attended Oberlin College in Ohio and worked with several of Brown's men on the convention's final arrangements. Anderson would later join Brown's raiders.

Brown also met Harriet Tubman, one of the leaders of the Underground Railroad. Tubman gave Brown what information she had about the Virginia terrain and what allies he might find there.

DELAYS

In March 1857, Brown had hired Hugh Forbes to train his men. Forbes was an English soldier of fortune who had gained military experience while fighting with Garibaldi in Italy. In Iowa in August 1857, Forbes and Brown put together a plan for fighting slavery in the South. The two men quarreled over many of the details. Forbes continued working with Brown's men, but he grew angry with Brown for not giving him more money and authority. In January 1858, Forbes left Iowa for Washington, D.C., and revealed Brown's plan to several politicians.

No one in power really believed Forbes. The Secret Six, however, received threatening letters from him and feared that the authorities would discover who they were. A nervous Gerrit Smith wanted to cut off all connections with Brown. "I never was convinced of the wisdom of this scheme," Smith said, "but as things now stand, it seems to me it would be madness to attempt to execute it." Others in the group suggested postponing the raid. Thomas Higginson and Samuel Howe wanted no delays. "I regard any postponement as simply abandoning the project," said Higginson, "for if we give it up now at the command or threat of Hugh Forbes, it will be the same next year . . . I protest against postponement." Nonetheless, George Stearns and Gerrit Smith, who supported a delay in plans, supplied most of the money and their words carried more weight. So the group voted to delay Brown's raid.

The group then made a new "blind" arrangement with Brown. They told Brown not to provide the members with any further information of his plans. That way, no one could charge them with a crime. As Smith wrote Franklin Sanborn, "I do not wish to know Captain Brown's plans; I hope he will keep them to himself." After June 1858, Brown's supporters in the East probably had little definite knowledge of his activities or plans.

To satisfy the Secret Six, Brown agreed to go to Kansas as a diversion. The trip would make Forbes's accusations of a Virginia raid look foolish. Unfortunately, this meant disbanding his small group of followers in Springdale. Most of them scattered to Ohio, Illinois, and Iowa, promising to reassemble when Brown called them. Some abandoned Brown and his project forever.

Aaron Stevens agreed to raise money in Iowa and then rejoin Brown in Kansas. John Cook went to Harpers Ferry as a spy. Brown asked him to find out everything he could about the people in the area and the layout of the government arsenal. Brown set off for Kansas with John Kagi and Charles Tidd.

RUNNING OFF SLAVES

Conditions in Kansas had changed since 1856. Antislavery settlers now controlled the territorial legislature and were majorities in most counties. In August 1858, while Brown waited, settlers flocked to the polls and rejected the proslavery constitution by a vote of 11,300 to 1,788. The struggle over slavery in Kansas was over, although Southern politicians prevented Kansas from joining the United States until after the Civil War began.

The environment in Kansas, however, was not completely calm. In May 1858, a proslavery party had kidnapped 11 people from Linn County, marched them to a gully, and shot them in cold blood. Five antislavery settlers died and the remainder were wounded. As usual, the authorities declined to prosecute or even pursue the 20 vigilante killers. Brown was determined to retaliate.

In December 1858, Brown, along with Kagi, Tidd, and Stevens, led a raiding party into Missouri. The raiding force included two new recruits, Indiana native Jeremiah Goldsmith

Albert Hazlett was one of John Brown's followers. After escaping from Harpers Ferry, he changed his name to William H. Harrison and the raid survivors pretended not to know him. His plan failed and he was captured and hanged on March 16, 1860.

Anderson and Pennsylvanian Albert Hazlett. Hazlett had moved to Kansas in the winter of 1856–1857 and fought in free-state guerrilla forces. Anderson had already been arrested twice by proslavery forces.

Brown's raiders attacked two proslavery homesteads in Missouri, confiscated horses and wagons, liberated 11 slaves, and took 2 white men captive. For Brown, the attack boosted his hopes for his larger planned raid in Virginia. Still, Brown's lawless actions angered many antislavery settlers. Now that Free Staters were in control of Kansas, they had nothing to gain by angering their slaveholding neighbors.

Nonetheless, Brown now had 11 freed slaves in his care, including a pregnant woman. For a month, the fugitives hid in an abandoned cabin near Pottawatomie Creek. In January 1859, Brown began a long journey to take the liberated slaves to Detroit and then on to Canada. The group marched through Kansas, Nebraska, Iowa, Illinois, Indiana, and Michigan in the middle of a bitter prairie winter. Through a combination of skill and luck, they avoided capture. On March 12, 1859, after 82 days and more than 1,000 miles of hard travel, Brown saw the rescued group off on a ferry bound for freedom in Canada.

THE MAN TO DO THE DEED

Over the next few months, Brown traveled again through the East trying to drum up support for the cause. In May 1859, he delivered a lecture in Concord, Massachusetts, attended by Emerson, Thoreau, and educator Bronson Alcott. That night, Alcott wrote in his journal, "The captain leaves us much in the dark concerning his destination and designs for the coming months. Yet . . . I think him equal to anything he dares—the man to do the deed, if it must be done. . . ."

Brown also met with members of the Secret Six. They contributed more than $2,000, with Stearns alone giving $1,200. Samuel Gridley Howe reminded Brown, "Don't tell me what you are about to do or where you are going."

On June 11, Brown visited his family in North Elba. His son Watson agreed to join him, but Jason and Salmon decided not to go south. Salmon told his father that, "the trip was a mistake . . . it was not the wise thing to do." Brown urged and browbeat Salmon, but the son could be as stubborn as the old man. Brown was bitterly disappointed. He told his wife that he regretted Salmon's decision as he "had never regretted the act of any of his children."

On June 16, 1859, Brown told his family good-bye and rode out of the Adirondacks for the last time. With him were five members of the North Elba community: his sons Owen, Oliver, and Watson, along with William and Dauphin Thompson, brothers of his son-in-law Henry. All were committed to Brown's war against slavery.

THE KENNEDY FARM

On July 3, 1859, Brown and his sons Owen and Oliver, and Jeremiah Anderson arrived by train at Sandy Hook, Maryland. This was a small village about a mile from Harpers Ferry. They were searching for a staging area for their intended raid. The four men presented themselves as Isaac Smith & Sons, cattle-men from New York. They claimed to be looking for a small farm to serve as a feeding lot for cattle. Robert Kennedy, who had died earlier in the year, had owned a farm in the area. Brown rented the empty and unfurnished place from the trustee of Kennedy's estate for $35 in gold. Brown and his fol-lowers would spend about four months at the Kennedy farm in the summer of 1859.

Now Brown waited for the arrival of his recruits. Unfortunately for him, they never appeared in the numbers he expected. The so-called Provisional Army of the United States straggled in, one or two at a time, throughout the sum-mer months. Brown was hoping for 50 recruits. In the end, he would have only 21 men (16 whites and 5 blacks).

Twelve of the raiders had fought with Brown in Kansas. The oldest of the band, after Brown, was Dangerfield Newby, age 44. Owen Brown came next, at 35; all the others were under 30. Oliver Brown, Barclay Coppoc, and William Leeman were not even 21. Some, such as Brown's sons Watson and Oliver, had only recently married. "I would gladly come home and stay with you always," Watson wrote his wife, Belle, "but for the cause which brought me here—a desire to do something for others, and not live wholly for my own happiness."

Brown sent for his 15-year-old daughter, Annie, and 17-year-old daughter-in-law, Martha (Oliver's wife), to help out and divert suspicion from the all-male household. Martha did the cooking and helped the men with the housework. Annie sat on the porch and made sure nosy neighbors did not drop by unexpectedly. The men often hid in the attic loft. They spent much of their time studying a manual of military tactics, reading, and debating.

At the end of September, Brown sent Annie and Martha home. It was increasingly difficult to keep the men's presence a

DANGERFIELD NEWBY

Dangerfield Newby was the oldest of Brown's raiders. Newby had been born a slave in 1815 but was freed by his white father. Newby married a slave who was still in bondage about 30 miles south of Harpers Ferry. He had been unable to purchase the freedom of his wife, Harriet, and seven children from their owner. By joining Brown, he hoped to free his family by force. Newby was killed at Harpers Ferry. Harriet's distressing letters, found on Newby's body after the raid, helped advance the abolitionist cause.

Dear Husband
I want you to buy me as soon as possible, for if you do not get me some body else will. . . . Dear Husband you [know] not the trouble I see; the last two years has ben [sic] like a

secret and no new recruits seemed to be arriving. Brown decided that, ready or not, he could not wait much longer. Fifteen boxes of Sharps rifles, revolvers, and ammunition from Ohio reached Chambersburg, Pennsylvania, on August 11. These were the weapons pledged to Brown by the Massachusetts Committee in January 1858. They were then transported to the Kennedy farm in an old wagon. In late September, the 1,000 pikes arrived from Connecticut.

Brown's men knew there was a good chance they would be killed. Yet in letter after letter to friends and family, they wrote about their desire to serve the nation and humanity. William Leeman, in his last letter to his mother, wrote, "Yes, mother, I am warring with slavery, the greatest curse that ever infested America. . . . I am in a good cause and I am not afraid." As Brown

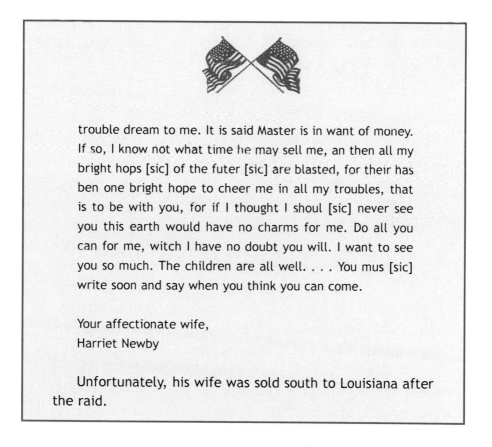

trouble dream to me. It is said Master is in want of money. If so, I know not what time he may sell me, an then all my bright hops [sic] of the futer [sic] are blasted, for their has ben one bright hope to cheer me in all my troubles, that is to be with you, for if I thought I shoul [sic] never see you this earth would have no charms for me. Do all you can for me, witch I have no doubt you will. I want to see you so much. The children are all well. . . . You mus [sic] write soon and say when you think you can come.

Your affectionate wife,
Harriet Newby

Unfortunately, his wife was sold south to Louisiana after the raid.

Nov. 26, 1859.] FRANK LESLIE'S ILLUSTRATED NEWSPAPER. 407

The Harper's Ferry Insurrection.

OLD JOHN BROWN'S RESIDENCE, KENNEDY FARM, MARYLAND.—FROM A SKETCH BY OUR OWN CORRESPONDENT.

Calling himself Isaac Smith, Brown rented the Kennedy Farm (shown in the newspaper above) for $35 in gold. Here, he trained and prepared his men for the raid on Harpers Ferry. Today, the farmhouse (located in present-day Sharpsburg, Maryland) has been restored and named a National Historic Landmark.

had told the men many times, "We have here only one life to live, and once to die; and if we lose our lives it will perhaps do more for the cause than our lives would be worth in any other way."

THE PLAN CHANGES AGAIN

Brown's original plan had been to establish a free state in the Appalachians. He had always thought that eventually he would raid the U.S. Arsenal at Harpers Ferry. The arsenal was a large complex of buildings that contained 100,000 muskets and rifles. With these weapons, Brown could arm the thousands of slaves he expected to rally to his support.

Now, however, he began to think about the dramatic effect of making an attack on the arsenal the first strike of the campaign. Of course, an attack on the U.S. Arsenal would bring government troops against him. Yet Brown had eluded them in Kansas and he felt he could do it again. If worse came to worst, Brown and his men could retreat into the wilds of the Blue Ridge Mountains.

After the raid, Brown gave confused and contradictory statements about his intentions. Several times, Brown said he did not want to incite a slave insurrection. Yet he also told his prisoners during the raid, and even the governor of Virginia, that he expected slave support. For what other purpose were the pikes and rifles?

Some of Brown's men still thought that they were going into Virginia on a large slave-running expedition. When Brown announced that they would begin by attacking and seizing a federal arsenal, they were thunderstruck. Brown's own sons, as well as Charles Tidd, argued that it was suicidal for a handful of men to capture and then hold a whole town against militia and possibly federal troops. Tidd kept repeating, "We shall be caught in a pen." Oliver argued that Harpers Ferry was an easy town to defend but also an easy place to be trapped and cut to pieces.

Once again, Brown had to convince his own men. He had help from Kagi and Cook, both of whom supported the plan. Finally, Oliver, Owen, and Watson decided they would follow wherever their father led. "We must not let our father die alone," Oliver declared. The other men agreed with the new plan.

"IT'S A PERFECT STEEL TRAP"

Brown still had one more person he wanted to convince to fight at his side. Brown and Frederick Douglass had been friends for more than a decade. Douglass had never met a white man so relentless in his opposition to slavery. Douglass recalled that Brown "thought that slaveholders had forfeited their right to live." Brown believed that Douglass would join him.

On August 19, Brown and John Kagi slipped away from the farm and met with Douglass and Shields Green at an abandoned stone quarry outside of Chambersburg. Brown described the planned raid in detail. He was dismayed when Douglass told him, "It's a perfect steel trap, John."

"Come with me, Douglass," Brown begged. "When I strike, the bees will begin to swarm, and I shall want you to help hive them." Brown's plea moved Douglass, but he still believed the plan was foolish. Douglass "opposed it with all the arguments at my command. . . . It would be an attack on the Federal Government, and would array the whole country against us." Brown told Douglass he would be able to dictate a term for safe passage out of town because he would have hostages. Douglass replied that Virginia would "blow him and his hostages sky-high rather than that he should hold Harpers Ferry an hour."

Brown continued for two days to attempt to persuade Douglass to join his force, but Douglass refused. Before leaving, Douglass asked Shields Green if he wished to return to Rochester or join Brown. Green replied, "I believe I'll go with the old man." Douglass returned to Rochester alone. It was the last time he would see his old friend. He would later write, "His zeal in the cause of freedom was infinitely superior to mine—it was as the burning sun to my taper light. . . . I could live for the slave; John Brown could *die* for him."

BROWN'S LAST RECRUITS

John Kagi recruited Lewis Leary and John Copeland in Cleveland in September 1859. Leary was a free born African-American harness maker. In Oberlin, he was one of the men who took part in rescuing a runaway slave in an incident known as the Oberlin-Wellington rescue. Leary left a wife and a six-month-old child at Oberlin when he joined Brown. She did not know of his plans.

Copeland was born in Raleigh, North Carolina. In 1842, Copeland moved north to Ohio. He attended college at Oberlin and became involved in antislavery activities. He also participated in the Oberlin-Wellington rescue. Copeland said he joined Brown "to assist in giving that freedom to at least a few of my poor and enslaved brethren who have been most foully and unjustly deprived of their liberty."

Brown's last recruit, Francis Merriam, reached the farm on October 15. Merriam was frail, one-eyed, and emotionally unbalanced. He had once visited Haiti and now wanted to help in "stealing slaves down South." He was the nephew of a famous abolitionist and had a ferocious hatred for slavery. He had learned of Brown's plot in Boston. Merriam not only volunteered his services but also contributed $600 in gold. Brown viewed the gold as a sign that God wanted him to move.

When nightfall came on October 16, 1859, Brown gathered his men together. He told them, "Do not . . . take the life of any one, if you can possibly avoid it; but if it is necessary to take life in order to save your own, then make sure work of it." At 8 P.M., Brown told the raiders, "Men, get on your arms; we will proceed to the Ferry!"

Harpers Ferry

The Harpers Ferry arsenal was built on a narrow strip of land in the Blue Ridge Mountains of northwestern Virginia. It was about 60 miles west of Baltimore and Washington, D.C. The town is located where the Shenandoah and Potomac rivers merge. On a nearby island in the Shenandoah River was Hall's Rifle Works, where gunsmiths made 10,000 weapons a year for the U.S. Army. In 1859, Harpers Ferry had a population of about 2,500, including about 1,250 free blacks and 88 slaves. There were no large plantations in the area. The climate was too cold and the land too mountainous for growing tobacco or cotton on a large scale.

On the chilly and overcast night of October 16, 1859, Brown assigned Francis Merriam, Owen Brown, and Barclay Coppoc to guard the farmhouse. John Cook and Charles Tidd, the raiders most familiar with the surrounding countryside, led

ATTACK ON THE INSURGENTS AT THE BRIDGE BY THE RAILROAD MEN.—FROM A SKETCH BY OUR OWN ARTIST.

This illustration depicts Brown's men attacking the railroad bridge that connected Maryland with Harpers Ferry. Initially the scheme started off with no problems, but later a railroad employee was shot and killed by one of Brown's men. Ironically, the victim was a free black man.

the way from Maryland to Harpers Ferry. As soon as possible, they cut the telegraph wires leading in and out of the town. At about 10 P.M., the men followed Brown onto the covered railroad bridge that led across the Potomac River into the town. Each man carried a knife, a revolver, a rifle, and about 40 rounds of ammunition.

Initially, the raid went very well. John Kagi and Aaron Stevens dashed onto the covered bridge and took the guard prisoner. John Brown left Watson Brown and Stewart Taylor behind on guard duty. The raiders met no resistance entering the town. They easily captured the U.S. Arsenal, which was defended only by a single guard. "I came here from Kansas, and this is a slave state," Brown supposedly told the frightened guard. "I want to free all the Negroes in this state; I have possession now of the

United States armory, and if the citizens interfere with me, I must only burn the town and have blood."

John Brown, Edwin Coppoc, and Albert Hazlett stood guard at the armory while the remaining men rushed to their assignments in different parts of town. Kagi and John Copeland took control of the rifle works a half-mile away at the other

THE HARPERS FERRY ARSENAL AND MASS PRODUCTION

In the 1790s, the U.S. government built two national arsenals. Secretary of War Henry Knox, a resident of Massachusetts, sponsored Springfield, Massachusetts, as the location for the first arsenal. For the second, President George Washington chose a remote location at Harpers Ferry, Virginia. Perhaps intentionally, Washington had placed one arsenal in the North and one in the South.

The arsenal at Harpers Ferry began producing muskets in about 1800. By 1816, it was turning out nearly 10,000 arms a year. The arsenal became a major contributor to the development of modern production methods. The chief innovator was John H. Hall, originally a Maine cabinetmaker and boatbuilder. In 1819, the U.S. War Department hired Hall to produce 1,000 rifles at Harpers Ferry. To do the job, the Yankee inventor developed new metalworking and woodworking machines. Hall also pioneered the use of precision gauges and measuring devices to make sure all parts came out the same. When he completed the contract in 1824, Hall proudly wrote to Secretary of War John Calhoun, "I have succeeded in an object which had hitherto completely baffled . . . those who have heretofore attempted it—I have succeeded in establishing methods for fabricating end of town. Oliver Brown and William Thompson seized the Shenandoah wagon bridge about 300 yards from the covered bridge. Some raiders also rounded up hostages from nearby farms. One of the hostages was Lewis Washington, the area's most distinguished citizen. Washington was a small but prosperous planter and the great grand nephew of George Washington.

arms exactly alike, and with economy, by the hands of common workmen. . . ." A committee established by the U.S. Congress confirmed all of Hall's claims in 1827.

In 1855, a commission of British manufacturers visited the United States to examine the advantages of the American manufacturing system. The British singled out Springfield and Harpers Ferry as examples of the new manufacturing system. The commission observed, "hundreds of valuable instruments and gauges that are employed . . . the object of all being to secure thorough identity in all parts."

In this way, Harpers Ferry played a key role in developing American industry. In 1800, a gun had been made by a few highly skilled artisans who had trained for years. Each gun was a handcrafted object. If a gun broke, it needed to be returned to its maker or another gunsmith who could shape and fit the unique replacement piece. The new system at Harpers Ferry made craft almost irrelevant. Unskilled workers now manufactured each part of the gun in large quantities with the help of complex machinery. The thousands of copies of each part were almost identical. If a piece broke, another could simply be substituted. The use of specific machinery and interchangeable parts at Harpers Ferry were components of one of the greatest contributions to world technology in the nineteenth century.

The men also spread the news to the local slaves that they were free. Osborne Anderson remembered that, "on the road, we met some colored men, to whom we made known our purpose, when they immediately agreed to join us. They said they had been long waiting an opportunity of the kind."

By midnight, just two hours after they entered Harpers Ferry, Brown and his men had captured the arsenal, rifle works, and the two bridges into town. Osborne Anderson marveled that the provisional army had accomplished it "without the snap of a gun, or any violence whatsoever." It was the perfect start.

THE TRAIN

Things started to go wrong for the provisional army at about 1 A.M. At that time, Brown's men fired at a relief security guard on the railroad bridge. Shortly afterward, an eastbound Baltimore and Ohio train approached the town. Hayward Shepperd, the train's baggage master, was a free black man. Shepperd may have tried to warn the passengers that there was trouble ahead. Brown's men yelled for him to halt and then, either Watson Brown or Stewart Taylor, opened fire and killed him. Ironically, a free black man became the first casualty of John Brown's war against slavery.

For some reason, Brown allowed the train to continue on its way. This wiped out any advantage gained by cutting the telegraph wires. Soon rumor passed for fact and hysteria reigned supreme in the Virginia and Maryland countryside. At 11:30 A.M., the *Alexandria Gazette* reported that, "there were not less than from 250 to 300 of the insurgents. They had arrested every citizen they could find." Newspaper reports shrieked, "Fire and Rapine on the Virginia Border," and "Negro Insurrection at Harper's Ferry."

By early morning, the townspeople of Harpers Ferry were aroused. The shots and the commotion around the armory and in the streets fed rumors of a massive slave revolt. The town sent out messengers and alarm bells rang in nearby Charlestown, Martinsburg, and Shepherdstown. Southern volunteer militias, whose main purpose was to control slaves, began to assemble and head to Harpers Ferry.

DELAY

In the meantime, John Brown did not seem to be in any rush to leave Harpers Ferry. Brown took the time to order breakfast from a local hotel for his men and the hostages. He also spent valuable time trying to convince his prisoners that slavery was immoral. One hostage later testified, "During the day and night I talked much with Brown. I found him as brave a man could be, and sensible upon all subjects except slavery. Upon that question, he was a religious fanatic, and believed it was his duty to free the slaves, even if in doing so he lost his own life."

Meanwhile, local farmers, shopkeepers, and militia pinned down the raiders in the armory by firing from the heights behind the town. Brown's men returned fire and shot some of the local men. Half a mile away at the rifle works, Kagi observed the growing number of defenders in the hills above the town. He sent urgent messages to Brown urging that the scattered force leave the town before they lost the chance. Osborne Anderson remembered that Brown told Kagi "to hold out a few minutes longer, when we would all evacuate the place. Those few minutes proved disastrous, for then it was that the troops . . . came pouring in, increased by crowds of men from the surrounding countryside."

Brown was surprised by how quickly opposing forces had been mobilized in the countryside. He was not in Kansas anymore; Southerners in Virginia had been dreading and preparing for a slave uprising since Nat Turner's rebellion in 1831. Brown and his men had many chances to gather their hostages and government weapons and make a run for it. Yet the man of action seemed strangely paralyzed. After the raid, Brown offered a curious explanation for his delay: "I should have gone away; but

I had thirty-odd prisoners, whose wives and daughters were in tears for their safety, and I felt for them. Besides, I wanted to allay the fears of those who believed we came here to burn and kill. For this reason, I allowed the train to cross the bridge."

SURROUNDED

At about noon, a company of militia arrived from nearby Charlestown. Brown and several of his men tried to stop them from taking the Potomac and Shenandoah bridges. After a fierce battle, in which Dangerfield Newby became the first raider to die, the militia seized the bridges. This blocked Brown's only escape route back to his rear guard in Maryland.

The scattered forces of the provisional army were completely isolated from each other. Kagi, Copeland, and Leary faced intense fire at the rifle works. Hazlett and Osborne Anderson held out at the arsenal. Cook and Tidd were moving weapons and supplies to the schoolhouse outside of town.

Brown knew that he was trapped. He told the remaining raiders, "We will hold on to our three positions, if they are unwilling to come to terms, and die like men." Brown took the most important prisoners and remaining raiders into the engine house, a small brick building at the entrance to the armory. He had the doors and windows barred and loopholes cut through the brick walls. Brown and his raiders now faced the fire of hundreds of men with more militia companies arriving by the hour. President Buchanan, receiving a report that 700 whites and blacks were in the invasion force, ordered 3 artillery companies and 90 Marines to Harpers Ferry.

In the mid-afternoon, a large force of militia and townspeople attacked the rifle works. Kagi, Copeland, Leary, and two of the slaves who had joined them were driven out of the building. They had no choice but to try to flee by crossing the Shenandoah River. Kagi and the two slaves were killed almost immediately. Leary was badly wounded by several shots while trying to swim across the river. He was captured, but died eight hours later.

Copeland was also captured from a large rock in the middle of the river. He was almost lynched, but lived to stand trial.

CAPTURED

Thousands of shots now rained into the engine house. The bullets shattered every window and penetrated the walls. In three separate incidents, Brown sent his son Watson, William Thompson, and Aaron Stevens out under a white flag. Each time, the angry crowd refused to honor the flag of truce and shot them anyway. The crowd then took the injured Thompson and killed him in cold blood.

Random shooting followed all afternoon. Inside the engine house, Stewart Taylor lay near the doorway where he had been shot dead. Oliver Brown was badly wounded. He and Watson were both groaning in agony on the floor. Oliver begged his father to kill him and end his suffering. Brown told him, "If you must die, die like a man." A few minutes later, Oliver was dead. Yet, not when his sons died, nor at any other moment during the siege, did Brown or any of his men threaten or harm their hostages.

At the schoolhouse, John Cook, Owen Brown, Barclay Coppoc, Charles Tidd, and Francis Merriam received word that the situation was hopeless and decided to make a run for it. Osborne Anderson and Albert Hazlett, watching the arrival of hundreds of militia, also decided to escape from the arsenal while they could. Hazlett was later captured but Anderson eluded his pursuers and fled to Canada.

Somehow, Brown and a few men continued to hold off hundreds of Southern militia. But now it was a cold and pitch-dark night inside the engine house. Brown, four uninjured raiders—Edwin Coppoc, Jeremiah Anderson, Dauphin Thompson, and Shields Green—and 11 prisoners watched the night drag by. Throughout the long night, Brown treated his prisoners with courtesy. This astounded one of the hostages, who noted that Brown's sons had been "shot down beside him,

THE STORMING OF THE ENGINE-HOUSE BY THE UNITED STATES MARINES.—[SKETCHED BY PORTE CRAYON.]

Local farmers, shopkeepers, and militia were called in to fight Brown and his men. By the morning of October 18, the engine house, later known as John Brown's fort, was surrounded by Colonel Robert E. Lee's company of Marines. Using sledgehammers and battering rams to break down the doors, in just three minutes, Brown and his surviving men were captured.

[and] almost any other man similarly placed would at least have exacted life for life."

By the morning of October 18, a company of U.S. Marines under the command of Colonel Robert E. Lee surrounded the engine house. A young Army lieutenant, J.E.B. Stuart, approached under a white flag. He told the raiders that their lives would be spared if they surrendered without any conditions. Brown refused, saying, "No, I prefer to die here."

The Marines then used sledgehammers and a battering ram to break down the engine room door. The hostage Lewis Washington called Brown "the coolest man I ever say in defying danger and death. With one son dead by his side, and another shot through, he felt the pulse of his dying son with one hand,

and held his rifle with the other, and commanded his men with the utmost composure, encouraging them to . . . sell their lives as dearly as they could."

Dauphin Thompson and Jeremiah Anderson were both bayoneted and killed. Lieutenant Israel Greene cornered Brown and struck him in the head several times with a sword, wounding him. Greene thrust his sword toward Brown's stomach, but the sword apparently hit Brown's belt buckle and bent. Greene

SHIELDS GREEN: I GUESS I'LL GO BACK WITH THE OLD MAN

Shortly after Albert Hazlett and Osborne Anderson decided to flee the arsenal, they met Shields Green. During the raid, Green had been recruiting slaves from the nearby countryside to join the fighting.

Anderson told Green that they were escaping. He begged Green to come with them. Green looked back at the engine house.

"You think there's no chance, Osborne?"

"Not one," Anderson replied.

"And the old Captain can't get away?"

"No," Anderson and Hazlett both replied.

"Well," said Green slowly. "I guess I'll go back with the old man."

And so, though he had a chance to escape capture, Shields Green returned to the fighting. He was captured with Brown in the engine house.

Looking back, Anderson later said, "Wiser and better men no doubt there were, but a braver man never lived than Shields Green."

then beat Brown across the head with the hilt of his sword and Brown fell unconscious. The attack was over in about three minutes. One Marine was killed and one wounded. John Brown was now a captive.

JUDGMENT

John Brown, as a Calvinist, believed that in the end, everything was predestined. The only thing a truly religious person could do was to trust in God. Possibly for this reason, Brown never did enough advance work for his raid. He made no effort to alert free blacks or slaves he was coming. He did not scout the area to find trails and hidden places of refuge. Nor did he bother to work out an escape plan.

At least 80 people knew about Brown's projected invasion. Many others had good reason to believe that Brown was planning some outrageous move in Virginia. Yet somehow, Brown's raid caught everyone by surprise. In the first two hours, without firing a shot, he took the town, hostages, armory, and arsenal.

If Brown had taken the necessary firearms and headed for the hills, any one of a hundred possible outcomes could have occurred. His New England backers thought this was his intention. John Kagi kept urging him to leave. Instead, Brown delayed so long with his hostages that white Southerners surrounded, rushed, and captured him.

Brown's reasons for delay are still not entirely clear. Yet it is unmistakable that Brown lacked a definite plan for his invasion. He never recruited enough men, and then dispersed his small force throughout the town. He cut himself off from his base of support and failed to keep open his only avenues of retreat. In the end, most of Brown's men were caught in "the perfect steel trap" predicted by Frederick Douglass.

Altogether, Brown's men killed five people and wounded nine. Among the dead was the mayor of Harpers Ferry and one of Colonel Lee's soldiers. Ten of Brown's men died,

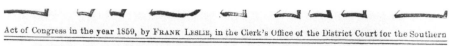

Act of Congress in the year 1859, by FRANK LESLIE, in the Clerk's Office of the District Court for the Southern

NEW YORK, SATURDAY, NOVEMBER 5, 1859.

HARPER'S FERRY INSURRECTION—BURYING THE DEAD INSURGENTS.

Ten of Brown's men were killed, including two of his sons. Five escaped, and seven of his raiders, including Brown, were captured and arrested. Above is a newspaper illustration depicting the burial of Brown's men.

including his sons Watson and Oliver. Seven men, including the rearguard, had escaped. Hazlett and Cook were captured while fleeing through Pennsylvania the following week. The remaining five escapees—Owen Brown, Frances Merriam,

Charles Tidd, Barclay Coppoc, and Osborne Anderson—all escaped for good. By sheer luck, John Brown was not killed in the final minutes. Had he died, his story would have turned out very differently.

SLAVES AND REBELLION

Brown had only 21 men. His plan counted on the support of thousands of slaves to rise and join him. Yet the events of the raid challenged Brown's long-held belief that blacks would rise up with determination if they had the chance. Most blacks in the Harpers Ferry area seem to have reacted with indifference or fear. No slave uprisings took place anywhere in Virginia and Maryland. A local paper crowed after the raid, "Brown's expectation as to slaves rushing to him, was entirely disappointed. None seem to have come to him willingly, and in most cases were forced to desert their masters."

Most of the handful of slaves that Brown freed had refused to fight back once the shooting began around the armory. Lewis Washington said in court "that not a slave had a heart in the matter. The slaves themselves did nothing." The slaves liberated from Colonel Washington's plantation on Sunday night returned to their homes after the raid's failure. They swore that they had been compelled by Brown's men to escape, for they knew they might be burned alive if guilty of insurrection.

Black abolitionists such as Frederick Douglass and Henry Highland Garnet had warned Brown that the slaves would be slow to rebel or flee. Southern slaves lacked organization and were suspicious of white leadership. They had little or no knowledge of the details of Brown's raid. They did know that a certain and horrible death awaited them if the raid failed. Slaves had learned, from experience, to be practical. They refused to throw away their lives until Brown's raid showed some signs of success. For all these reasons, the slaves had been unable and unwilling to join Brown.

Of course, white Southerners offered a racist argument. Edmund Ruffin boasted of the "submission, obedience, and general loyalty of our negro slaves." Yet underneath their boasting, Southerners were terrified. They, too, thought the slaves would rush to rebel. Hysterical eyewitness reports had converted five armed black men into 500. Everyone in the South immediately believed these reports. Only after the collapse of the raid did Southerners claim that they were confident that their slaves were content.

Brown's war for slave liberation ended only 36 hours after it began. On Tuesday afternoon, October 18, 1859, it seemed as though Brown's campaign to end American slavery had ended in dismal failure. Yet perhaps his defeat and death could yield another kind of victory.

I, John Brown

John Brown, bloody and unconscious, was moved to the floor of an office in a nearby armory. Within hours, Virginia governor Henry Wise, Virginia senator James Mason, and pro-Southern representative Clement Vallandigham of Ohio arrived in Harpers Ferry. Amazingly, they decided to question Brown immediately.

Brown lay on a rough pallet on the floor. He had not slept in nearly 60 hours. His hair was streaked and clotted with blood. He had barely eaten in two days. Yet Brown, going in and out of consciousness, said he would gladly answer questions because "he wanted to make himself and his motives clearly understood." Dozens of questions were hurled at the injured man. "In the midst of his enemies," wrote a reporter for a Baltimore newspaper, "with the gallows staring him full in the face, he lay

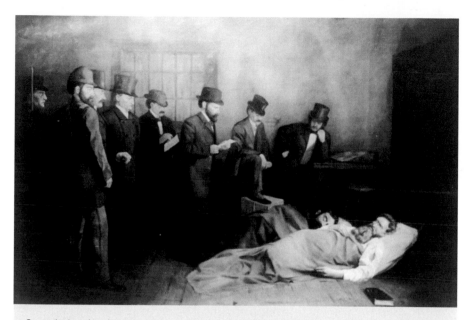

Struck in the head several times with a sword, Brown went in and out of consciousness while being questioned about his role in the raid. Still, a doctor pronounced him fit for trial. He and his men were held in the office of the arsenal.

on the floor, and in reply to every question, gave answers that betokened the spirit that animated him."

James Mason led the questioning, which lasted a full three hours. Despite his weakness, Brown was still very careful about his answers. He absolutely refused to give the identities of anyone who had helped him. When Mason asked him the key question—"What was your object in coming?"—Brown replied, "We came to free the slaves, and only that . . . I think, my friend, you are guilty of a great wrong against God and humanity . . . and it would be perfectly right for anyone to interfere with you so far as to free those you willfully and wickedly hold in bondage."

He also told his questioners that, "I don't think the people of the slave states will ever consider the subject of slavery in its true light till some other argument is resorted to than moral persuasion." In some answers, he was either dishonest or confused. When Vallandigham asked him if he expected "a general rising of the slaves in case of your success," Brown replied, "No, sir; nor did I wish it. I expected to gather them up from time to time and set them free."

One of Brown's best exchanges was with an unnamed bystander:

Bystander: "Do you consider this a religious movement?"

Brown: "It is, in my opinion, the greatest service man can render to God."

Bystander: "Do you consider yourself an instrument in the hands of Providence?"

Brown: "I do."

Bystander: "Upon what principle do you justify your acts?"

Brown: "Upon the Golden Rule. I pity the poor in bondage that have none to help them: that is why I am here; not to gratify any personal animosity, revenge, or vindictive spirit. It is my sympathy with the oppressed and the wronged that are as good as you and as precious in the sight of God."

Finally, Brown grew tired. A writer from the *New York Herald* offered to print a final statement. Brown concluded by saying, "You may dispose of me very easily—I am nearly disposed of now; but this question is still to be settled—this Negro question I mean: the end of that is not yet."

THE TRIAL

Brown had always demanded action and ridiculed talk. Ironically, Brown himself failed in military action but succeeded in the way he talked. After his capture, Brown turned himself into an antislavery symbol. "I have been whipped as the saying is," he wrote his wife, "but I am sure I can recover all the lost capital occasioned by that disaster; by only hanging a few moments by the neck; and I feel quite determined to make the utmost possible out of a defeat." He would win the battle not with bullets but with words.

The Marines had moved Brown and the other captives to a jail in Charlestown, the county seat about eight miles from Harpers Ferry. Brown's attack had taken place on federal property and any trial should have taken place in federal court. Instead, Governor Wise ordered that the raiders' trial take place in a Virginia state court already meeting in Charlestown within a few days.

Brown's trial began on October 27, only 10 days after the raid. Virginia authorities feared that angry Southerners would lynch Brown or that determined abolitionists would help him escape. The speed of the trial outraged many people, but it was legal under Virginia law.

Reporters and townspeople packed the courtroom, which was now the focus of the nation. Brown, still suffering from his wounds, was charged with murder, conspiring with slaves to rebel, and committing treason against Virginia. A doctor pronounced Brown physically fit for trial. Judge Richard Parker ordered the jury to be fair and "not allow their hatred of abolitionists to influence them. . . ."

The court assigned two Virginia lawyers to Brown. They promptly tried to claim that Brown was insane. His lawyers hoped to help Brown escape hanging by having him placed in an asylum; however, Brown refused to support any claims of insanity and the issue never came up again in court.

By midweek, two antislavery Boston lawyers arrived in Charlestown to take over the case. Still, Brown's position was fairly hopeless. Witnesses described the seizure of the buildings, the wounding and killing of several people, and the involvement of both free and enslaved black men in the attacking party. Brown's provisional constitution, entered as evidence, implied that Brown wanted to overthrow the U.S. government and set up his own. Brown listened without emotion, lying back on a cot with his eyes closed.

Brown's defense concluded on October 31. His lawyer argued that Brown could not be guilty of treason against Virginia since he owed the state no loyalty in the first place. He

JOHN BROWN'S LAST SPEECH

On November 2, 1859, before his sentencing, the judge asked Brown if he had anything to say. Brown struggled to his feet and replied, "I have, may it please the court, a few words to say." His following few words, lasting a mere five minutes, are considered among the greatest speeches in American history. Thomas Wentworth Higginson called them "unequalled in the history of American oratory for simplicity and power." Ralph Waldo Emerson would later compare them favorably to Lincoln's Gettysburg Address. Below is an excerpt from Brown's majestic final speech to the court:

> Had I interfered . . . in behalf of the rich, the powerful, the intelligent, the so-called great, or in behalf of any of their friends . . . it would have been all right; and every man in this court would have deemed it an act worthy of reward rather than punishment.
>
> This court acknowledges, as I suppose, the validity of the law of God. I see a book kissed here which I suppose to be the Bible, or at least the New Testament. That teaches me that all things whatsoever I would that men should do to me, I should do even so to them. It teaches me, further, to remember them that are in bonds, as bound with them. I endeavored to act up to that instruction. . . . I believe that to have interfered as I have done as I have always freely admitted I have done in behalf of His despised poor, was not wrong, but right. Now, if it is deemed necessary that I should forfeit my life for the furtherance of the ends of justice, and mingle my blood further with the blood of my children and with the blood of millions in this slave country whose rights are disregarded by wicked, cruel, and unjust enactments, I submit; so let it be done!

emphasized that Brown had not killed anyone himself, that he had treated his prisoners kindly, and that his negotiators had been shot down while carrying a flag of truce.

Andrew Hunter presented the closing arguments for the prosecution. He argued that Brown's "provisional government was a real thing, and no debating society, as his counsel would have us believe." According to Hunter, Brown had intended to "usurp the government, manumit our slaves, confiscate the property of slaveholders . . . [and] take possession of the Commonwealth."

The trial lasted a week. On November 2, after only 45 minutes of deliberation, the Charlestown jury found John Brown guilty on all three counts. The court sentenced Brown to be executed by public hanging in one month.

BROWN'S FINAL LETTERS

Governor Wise had wanted Brown's trial to be short, and then to hang him in "double quick time." Unfortunately for Wise, even a month turned out to be not fast enough. During his time in jail, Brown was allowed to send and receive letters. In the first week after his conviction, he wrote very little. Then he began to write eloquent letters to family members, supporters, strangers, and newspaper editors. By his execution, Brown had written more than 100 letters explaining and justifying his actions at Harpers Ferry. Newspapers reprinted many of these letters and Brown won increasing numbers of supporters in the North.

Far from feeling gloomy or defeated, Brown's letters were accepting and even joyous. He felt he had done his life's work; now it was time to die. He often compared himself to the imprisoned Paul, the captive Samson, and even to Jesus Christ. "I can trust God with both the time and manner of my death," he wrote Mary on November 8, "believing as I now do, that for me at this time to seal my testimony for God and humanity with my blood will do vastly more toward advancing the cause

I have earnestly endeavored to promote than all I have done in my life before."

In another letter, he compared himself to the heroes of the American Revolution. He reminded his cousin that the American soldiers were also considered rebels at the time and that they "too might have perished on the scaffold had circum-stances been but very little different. The fact that a man dies under the hand of an executioner (or other wise) has little to do with his true character. . . . I neither feel mortified, degraded, nor in the least ashamed of my imprisonment, my chain, or my prospect of death by hanging."

Brown received so many visitors that his jailor, John Avis, had to bring them into the cell in groups. Avis and Brown formed a bond of mutual respect. In exchange for generous treatment from Avis, Brown promised he would not try to escape. Brown now preferred to die as a martyr. "I doubt if I ought to encourage any attempt to save my life," he said. "I may be wrong, but I think that my great object will be nearer its accomplishment by my death than by my life."

One thing did outrage him in jail. He refused any help from Southern ministers. "These ministers who profess to be Christian, and hold slaves or advocate slavery, I cannot abide," he wrote. "My knees will not bend in prayer with them while their hands are stained with the blood of souls."

Hundreds of letters poured into his cell. Brown carefully preserved all the letters that praised him but threw in the trash box the ones that told him he got what he deserved. He even received a gloating letter from Mahalia Doyle, whose husband and two sons Brown had executed along the Pottawatomie in 1856. The letter ended in the trash box.

John Brown tried to discourage Mary from visiting because it "would only add to my affliction; and cannot possibly do me any good." Yet she was determined to come and see him one more time. He did not forbid it. On December 1, his wife arrived at the Charlestown jail. They embraced, talked alone

EW YORK, SATURDAY, DECEMBER 17, 1859.

JOHN BROWN'S LAST INTERVIEW WITH HIS WIFE IN THE JAIL AT CHARLESTOWN, VA.

After a weeklong trial and 45 minutes deliberation, Brown was found guilty of treason against Virginia, the murder of four whites and a black, and conspiring with slaves to rebel. He was sentenced to be hanged in public. On December 1, 1859, his wife joined him for his last meal, as depicted in this illustration.

for several hours, and then shared a last meal with John Avis and his family. Governor Wise had denied her permission to stay for the night. This was the only time that Brown lost his temper throughout his entire ordeal. Still, his anger quickly passed and he was calm when he told Mary good-bye.

In a last letter to his family, he wrote, "I am awaiting the hour of my public murder with great composure of mind and cheerfulness, feeling the strong assurance that in no other possible way could I be used to so much advantage to the cause of good and of humanity, and that nothing that either I or all my family have sacrificed or suffered will be lost."

THE NOT-SO-SECRET-SIX PANIC

Unfortunately for Brown's financial backers in the North, investigators found incriminating documents in a carpetbag at the Kennedy farm. Brown had probably left them there intentionally. Should the raid fail, he intended to commit as many people to the struggle as possible, whether or not they wanted to be committed.

Suddenly, the identities of the Secret Six were not so secret. Virginia authorities began proceedings to bring Brown's supporters to trial. In the following weeks, members of the group burned their letters to and from Brown, sent lawyers to represent him in court, put together plots to break him out of jail, and decided if they should stay in the country or flee to safer shores.

Gerrit Smith either suffered or pretended to have a nervous breakdown. His family committed him to a month's care at the Utica Asylum in upstate New York. Samuel Gridley Howe and George Stearns took off for Canada and remained there until after Brown's execution. Franklin Sanborn twice fled to Canada, fearing he would be arrested at any moment. Each time he returned. Theodore Parker was in Rome, Italy, dying from tuberculosis; he would outlive Brown by only six months.

The only member of the Secret Six who absolutely refused to run was the fiery Thomas Wentworth Higginson. "Is there no such thing as honor among confederates?" he wrote Sanborn. Higginson remained in the United States, refusing even to burn the letters tying him to Brown. Higginson not only defied the authorities to arrest him, but he also planned several dramatic rescue schemes to save Brown. Fifty years later, he would write, "we were trying to do right. And I believe . . . we did do right. . . . My one perennial wish, however, is that we would have achieved that end without the sacrifice of Brown."

Frederick Douglass was speaking in Philadelphia when Brown's raid took place. Virginia authorities charged Douglass with murder, robbery, and inciting a slave rebellion. Douglass quickly returned home to Rochester and destroyed any incriminating papers connecting him to Brown. Then he fled to Canada just ahead of his pursuers. From there, Douglass went to England, where he had already scheduled a lecture tour. Safe from arrest, Douglass praised Brown, calling him "THE man of this nineteenth century."

SOUTHERN REACTION

The Harpers Ferry raid outraged almost all white Southerners. Editorials in Southern newspapers condemned Brown as an agent of Satan, a treasonous murderer who wished to destroy Southern society. "The rage for vengeance which is felt by the citizens of this place," cried the *Charleston [SC] Mercury*, "can only be fully and satisfactorily satisfied by the blood of John Brown."

Many white Southerners blamed the entire North for the raid. They believed, despite all the evidence to the contrary, that every Northerner was secretly an abolitionist fanatic who supported slave rebellions. *De Bow's Review*, a Southern journal, stated that the North had "sanctioned and applauded theft, murder, treason" and "has shed southern blood on southern soil! There is—there can be no peace."

Many white Southerners reasoned that since the entire North was against them, their best future action was to secede from the United States. *The Enquirer* of Richmond stated that, "the Harpers Ferry invasion has advanced the cause of Disunion more than any other event that has happened since the formation of the government." Southern secessionists realized immediately that Brown's raid would work to their benefit. Virginia's Edmund Ruffin, a supporter of secession, wrote in his journal on October 19 that an incident such as Harpers Ferry was "needed to stir the sluggish blood of the South."

Governor Wise of Virginia spoke for most Southern whites when he called Brown and his men "murderers, traitors, robbers, insurrectionists," and "wanton, malicious, unprovoked felons." Yet on another level, he respected John Brown and admitted that he had some admirable qualities. "They are themselves mistaken who take him to be a madman," Governor Wise said. "He is a man of clear head, of courage, fortitude. . . . He is cool collected, and indomitable . . . he inspired me with great trust in his integrity, as a man of truth. He is a fanatic, vain and garrulous, but firm, truthful, and intelligent." Some people warned Governor Wise that hanging the raiders would only make them martyrs in the North. Yet given popular opinion in the south, Wise thought he had no choice but to execute Brown for his crimes.

NORTHERN OPINION CHANGES

The North did not speak with one voice on Brown's raid on Harpers Ferry. At first, most Northerners did agree that Brown was a lunatic. Few people showed any sympathy at all. A Chicago newspaper called the raid "a stark-mad enterprise," the work of "a squad of fanatics . . . all commanded by a man who has, for years, been mad as a March hare." The best William Lloyd Garrison could say about Brown's raid in *The Liberator* was that it was "a misguided, wild, and apparently insane, though disinterested and well intended effort."

As Brown's trial progressed, and then as newspapers published his letters, thousands of Northerners came to admire his courage, faith, and ideals. Many readers agreed with the *New York Tribune*, which stated that Brown and his followers, "dared and died for what they felt to be right, though in a manner which seems to us fatally wrong."

THOREAU AND BROWN

Henry David Thoreau was a writer, naturalist, and philosopher. He was born in Concord, Massachusetts, in 1817. Through Ralph Waldo Emerson, Thoreau became involved in the transcendentalist movement. The transcendentalists emphasized individualism and critical thinking. Thoreau's journey of self-discovery led him to Walden Pond, near Concord, where he built a cabin and lived for two years. Out of this experience, Thoreau wrote *Walden*, one of his most famous works.

Thoreau hated slavery. In 1846, he spent a night in the Concord jail rather than pay his taxes to the government; he claimed they would use it to support slavery. As a result, Thoreau wrote the important essay known as "Civil Disobedience." In it, he argued that the individual should always follow his or her conscience rather than the majority or the government. If a law was "of such a nature that it requires you to be the agent of injustice to another," he wrote, "then, I say, break the law." The essay was a major influence on Mahatma Gandhi and Martin Luther King.

In Brown, Thoreau found a fellow believer in resistance to an unjust government's support of slavery. He spoke in Brown's defense almost immediately after the raid on Harpers Ferry. This placed him against popular opinion, which initially had condemned Brown. On October 30, 1859, Thoreau presented his essay, "A Plea for Captain John Brown," to the town of Concord. Thoreau praised Brown's commitment to justice and equality. He declared, "I would rather see a statue of Captain Brown in the Massachusetts State-House yard, than that of any other

(continues)

(continued)

man whom I know." Thoreau considered Brown's actions to be a form of civil disobedience. He wrote, "Is it not possible that an individual may be right and a government wrong? Are laws to be enforced simply because they were made? Or declared by any number of men to be good, if they are not good?"

On the morning of Brown's hanging, Thoreau declared, "Some 1800 years ago, Christ was crucified. This morning . . . Captain Brown was hung. . . . He is not Old Brown any longer; he is an angel of light." Thoreau only outlived him by three years.

Opinions began to change when Ralph Waldo Emerson applauded Brown's actions. Emerson was the United States's most popular lecturer and the country's leading intellectual. Americans respected his opinions. In lectures at Boston and Concord, Emerson called Brown "that new saint, than whom none purer or more brave was ever led by love of men into conflict and death,—the new saint awaiting his martyrdom, and who if he shall suffer, will make the gallows glorious like the Cross." Emerson's "gallows glorious" phrase astonished and inspired Brown's supporters at the same time it outraged his opponents.

Abolitionists defended Brown even though most of them opposed violence in theory. "His bearing since his capture and during his trial has been truly sublime," said William Lloyd Garrison, "and challenges for him all of human sympathy and respect." He later asked rhetorically, "Was John Brown justified in his attempt? Yes, if Washington was in his . . ." In Brooklyn, Wendell Phillips astonished an immense audience by announcing, "the lesson of the hour is insurrection." Brown, Phillips declared, "has twice as much right to hang Governor Wise as Governor Wise has to hang him." The feminist Jane Swisshelm praised Brown's courage and wrote, "Adieu, until we meet in that land where there are no tyrants and no slaves."

Brown received his greatest support from African Americans. Throughout the North, blacks held emotional prayer and sympathy meetings for Brown. Many black men and women sent letters of esteem or sympathy to him in jail. Some African Americans in Chicago offered to contribute material aid to his family. They wrote, "How could we be so ungrateful as to do less for one who has suffered, bled, and now ready to die for the cause?"

EXECUTION

On the morning of December 2, 1859, John Avis went to Brown's cell to escort the old man to the gallows. Brown read his Bible and wrote a final letter to his wife, which included his will. He left several items to his family, including his surveyor's compass and "my large old Bible, containing the family record." He also left $50 toward his debt to the New England Woolen Company. The 15-year-old obligation still troubled him. He presented Avis with his silver watch, a token of appreciation for the care he had received. Proceeding down the corridor, he stopped before the cells of Copeland, Green, Cook, Coppoc, and Stevens to say good-bye.

As he stepped out of the corridor onto the street, Brown handed the guard a note he had written that morning. His final written words turned out to be quite prophetic: "I, John Brown, am now quite certain that the crimes of this guilty land will never be purged away, but with blood. I had, as I now think, vainly flattered myself that without very much bloodshed it might be done."

For many years, people believed that as John Brown descended the steps of the jail, he bent over and kissed an

JOHN BROWN ASCENDING THE SCAFFOLD PREPARATORY TO BEING HANGED.—FROM A SKETCH BY OUR SPECIAL ARTIST.

While Brown was imprisoned, cadets from the Virginia Military Institute were assigned security detail in the event Brown's supporters attempted a rescue. Brown did not want to be rescued, though; he was ready to die as a martyr. On the morning of December 2, 1859, Brown was escorted through a crowd of soldiers and hanged. Among them were future Confederate general Thomas "Stonewall" Jackson and John Wilkes Booth, who borrowed a militia uniform in order to gain admission.

enslaved black child. This story had an irresistible appeal to Brown's supporters. It appeared in many speeches, poems, and essays on Brown. The most famous example is a poem by John Greenleaf Whittier entitled "Brown of Osawatomie," where the martyr "stooped between the jeering ranks and kissed the Negro child!" At least three artists painted the scene. Thomas Hovenden's painting "The Last Moments of John Brown" (1884) was reproduced as a Currier & Ives lithograph and spread the myth across the nation. The story, however, was absolutely untrue. Soldiers completely surrounded John Brown on the way to the gallows. No civilian, black or white, would have been able to get anywhere near him.

At 11 A.M., Brown mounted the back of a wagon where he took a seat on a long wooden box that would be his coffin. A column of soldiers escorted Brown to a field just outside of town. Governor Wise, fearing a last minute attempt to free Brown, had ordered nearly 3,000 soldiers to guard Charlestown. The elaborate security precautions proved unnecessary. In fact, many in the North would mock them as examples of Southern panic and cowardice.

Several persons who later became famous in the Civil War attended Brown's execution. Future Confederate general Thomas "Stonewall" Jackson stood with the cadets of the Virginia Military Institute. He saw only "unflinching firmness" in Brown's actions. Edmund Ruffin, who fired the first shots of the Civil War at Fort Sumter, wrote, "He is as thorough a fanatic as ever suffered martyrdom and a very brave and able man. It is impossible for me not to respect his thorough devotion to his bad cause." Also watching in the crowd was the actor John Wilkes Booth, who would later assassinate President Lincoln. Booth had borrowed a military uniform in order to view the execution. "I looked at the traitor and terrorizer with unlimited, undeniable contempt," wrote Booth.

Brown quickly mounted the steps to the gallows. Ruffin thought he looked more like "a willing assistant instead of the victim." No preacher was present, as Brown still refused the services of any Southern minister. A white linen hood was placed over Brown's head, and he was hanged at 11:15 A.M. without incident.

9

"John Brown's Body Lies A-moulderin' in the Grave"

Brown was executed on December 2, 1859. That day, Americans gathered to praise or to condemn Brown and his men. William Lloyd Garrison wrote, "In Boston, we have thought it would be a master-stroke of policy to urge the day of his execution as the day for a general public expression of sentiment with reference to the guilt and danger of slavery." Throughout the North, church bells tolled for John Brown.

Some black abolitionists called December 2 "Martyr Day." In Boston, African Americans closed their places of business and draped them in mourning cloth. African Americans in large cities and small towns paused to honor Brown on the day of his death. Charles Langston, a black antislavery leader, told 2,000 mourners in Cleveland that Brown had been "murdered by the American people, murdered in consequence" of the "union with slavery."

In the days that followed, however, counterdemonstrations against Brown were even larger. Thousands of Northerners, as well as Southerners, viewed Brown as a criminal. Speaker after speaker condemned Brown's motives and justified his hanging. A New York paper insisted that the great mass of Northerners remained "as uncorrupted with Negro equality doctrines as ever."

In Massachusetts, Henry Wadsworth Longfellow, the country's greatest poet, predicted that Brown's death would mark "the date of a new Revolution . . . Even now as I write, they are leading Old John Brown to execution in Virginia for attempting to rescue slaves!" Then Longfellow added prophetically, "This is sowing the wind to reap the whirlwind, which will come soon."

BURIAL IN NORTH ELBA

In the late afternoon, Brown's body was shipped to Harpers Ferry. It was then placed aboard a train to begin the long journey home. Brown's body passed through Baltimore, Philadelphia, New York City, Troy (New York), and then the Vermont towns of Rutland and Vergennes. In every city and town they passed through, crowds gathered in the streets and church bells tolled as the train rolled by. After four days, they arrived on the shores of Lake Champlain and crossed over to Elizabethtown, New York, where Brown's body began the final journey to North Elba. The wagon journeyed through the mountains and reached the farm on December 7. Mary, who had accompanied the body, greeted her daughters with "a burst of love and anguish."

The funeral was held the next day. Abolitionist activists J. Miller McKim and Wendell Phillips spoke at the service. "History will date Virginia Emancipation from Harpers Ferry," Phillips predicted. Then he used a simile appropriate to the Adirondacks. "So, when the tempest uproots a pine . . . it looks green for months—a year or two. John Brown has loosened the roots of the slave system; it only breathes—it does not live hereafter." Lyman Epps led his sons in the hymn, "Blow Ye the Trumpet, Blow" that Brown had sung with them so often:

> Blow ye the trumpet, blow
> Sweet is Thy work, my God, my King.
> I'll praise my Maker with my breath.
> O, happy is the man who hears.
> Why should we start, and fear to die.
> With songs and honors sounding loud.
> Ah, lovely appearance of death.

Men next carried the coffin outside and lowered it into the frozen ground. His grave was near a great boulder that bore the name of Brown's grandfather, who fought in the American Revolution. Close by lay Frederick Brown, "murdered at Osawatomie for his adherence to the cause of freedom." Later, Brown's sons Oliver and Watson would be returned from Virginia and buried nearby. John Brown was buried "amid the silent, solemn, and snowy grandeur of the Adirondacks," with beautiful Lake Placid nearby and Whiteface Mountain looming over the grave.

MORE EXECUTIONS

Edwin Coppoc, John Cook, Shields Green, and John Copeland were all indicted and tried after Brown for treason against Virginia and other crimes. They were all found guilty and sentenced to death. On December 16, Green and Copeland were hung in the morning and Cook and Coppoc in the afternoon. None of them showed any signs of fear and all faced death with a calmness that impressed even their enemies.

Copeland wrote at least five letters while in prison. In his last letter, Copeland informed his family he did not fear the gallows because he felt he could not die for a more noble cause.

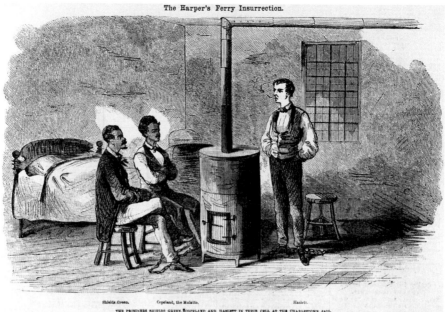

The Harper's Ferry Insurrection.

Shields Green. Copeland, the Mulatto. Hazlett.

THE PRISONERS SHIELDS GREEN, COPELAND AND HAZLETT IN THEIR CELL AT THE CHARLESTOWN JAIL.

Depicted are Shields Green, John Copeland, and Albert Hazlett in their cell at the Charlestown jail. They were charged with treason and murder and sentenced to hang. After the execution, the bodies of Green and Copeland (both black men) were dug up and taken to Winchester Medical College anatomy laboratory for dissection by students.

On the day of his death, Copeland wrote his family, "though we meet no more on earth, we shall meet in Heaven, where we shall not be parted by the demands of the cruel and unjust monster Slavery."

Coppoc wrote some Quaker friends in Iowa, "rest assured we shall not shame our dead companions by a shrinking fear. They lived and died like brave men. We, I trust, shall do the same." A journalist at the executions reported that Coppoc and Cook went up the scaffold's stairs "with a determined firmness that was scarcely surpassed by Captain Brown."

While the bodies of Coppoc and Cook were turned over to their families, Governor Wise refused to give up the bodies of the two black raiders. Instead, a group of medical students took their bodies to the Winchester Medical College for dissection. A family friend of Copeland's from Oberlin searched for his body. He said, "We visited the dissecting rooms. The body of Copeland was not there, but I was startled to find the body of another Oberlin neighbor whom I had often met upon our streets, a colored man named Shields Greene."

Albert Hazlett and Aaron Stevens went to trial on February 2, 1860, and were hung on March 16. They also met death as calmly as their companions. After his sentencing, Stevens wrote, "I am glad that I did not die of my wounds, for I believe that my execution upon the gallows will be a better testimony for truth and liberty." Likewise, Hazlett wrote the day before his hanging, "I am willing to die in the cause of liberty; if I had ten thousand lives, I would willingly lay them all down for the same cause." The bodies of Stevens and Hazlett were brought back to New Jersey for burial. Perth Amboy residents threatened to throw the coffins overboard on arrival, but abolitionists guarded the bodies and the burial proceeded quietly.

The courage with which Brown and his followers showed in the face of death was a source of pride for antislavery supporters in the North. The South, for all its boasting, did not seem to have a monopoly on chivalrous behavior. If anything, Virginia seemed rather cowardly, terrified by a small band of men who struck for freedom against great odds and died bravely.

THE REPUBLICAN PARTY

The Republican Party had replaced the Whig Party in 1854 after the passage of the Kansas-Nebraska Act. The Republicans were immediately successful, but they were a sectional party that drew all their strength from the North. Republicans stood for many things: a transcontinental railroad, cheap land in the West, and a high tariff. The Republican Party's main reason for existing was their opposition to the expansion of slavery. Republicans were usually not abolitionists. Most Republicans, such as Abraham Lincoln, could tolerate slavery where it already existed but were totally opposed to any expansion of slavery into the free West, such as in Kansas.

Brown despised the Republican Party. He thought it was far too conservative because it was not opposed to slavery every-where. Brown and his followers had no faith in the U.S. political system. They believed it was hopelessly corrupted by slavery. The Kansas-Nebraska Act and the *Dred Scott* decision seemed to confirm that belief.

Yet Northern and Southern Democrats tried to link Brown with the Republican Party. Stephen Douglas, U.S. senator from Illinois and soon to be the Democratic presidential can-didate, argued that the Harpers Ferry raid was the "natural, logical, inevitable result of the doctrines and teachings of the Republican Party." Many Northern newspapers agreed. The *New Hampshire Patriot* blamed the Harpers Ferry raid on "the principles and doctrine of arms and violence advocated by the black republican leaders. . . ." To their opponents, the party was always the "black Republicans," as if linking them to African Americans was enough in itself to discredit them.

Only two weeks after Brown's execution, the U.S. Senate appointed a five-person committee to investigate the Harpers Ferry raid. Its main purpose was to determine who contributed the arms, ammunition, or money to Brown. The three Democrats on the committee hoped to blame important Republicans for the raid. The two Republicans, on the other hand, tried to disas-sociate themselves from Brown and his acts.

The Senate committee heard testimony from 32 witnesses. The committee's report, written by Virginia senator James Mason (and signed by senator Jefferson Davis), turned out to be an enormous disappointment to everyone. It found no direct evidence of a conspiracy of organizations or individuals. The committee blamed only John Brown, stating that Brown was so secretive that "it does not appear that he entrusted even his immediate followers with his plans, fully, even after they were ripe for execution." The Democrats on the committee did claim that the Harpers Ferry raid directly resulted from Republican beliefs.

THE GREAT FEAR

The attack on Harpers Ferry spread panic throughout the South. Slavemasters may have claimed their slaves were loyal, but their actions belied their words. Fearing slave revolts from within and without, authorities strengthened their patrols, declared martial law, and terrorized any whites who expressed sympathy for blacks. The rights of free African Americans in the South were further restricted. In several Southern states, nervous citizens confiscated all books considered "anti-Southern" and destroyed them in ceremonial book burnings.

Brown's raid terrified not only Southern planters but the masses of nonslaveholding whites as well. Support for slavery became the definition of Southern patriotism even though only about one-third of Southern whites owned slaves. Small farmers and poor whites closed ranks behind slave owners to protect their homes from a supposed slave revolt.

After Harpers Ferry, white Southerners came to view the ownership of slaves as the basis of their entire way of life. Insane anxiety gripped the white population. Virginians bought more than 10,000 pistols in the days following the raid. Rumors spread of armed slaves gathering in the mountains.

Southerners transformed Brown into something he was not: a representative of the antislavery North. Mississippi senator Albert Gallatin Brown said, "Disguise it as you will, there is throughout all the non-slaveholding States of this Union a secret, deep-rooted sympathy with the object which this man had in view." The *Petersburg (Virginia) Express* simply drew the conclusion that "large portions of the North are our enemies." Governor Wise said, "the present relations between the states cannot be permitted longer to exist without abolishing slavery throughout the United States, or compelling us to defend it by force of arms. . . ." The raid on Harpers Ferry dramatically increased tensions between the North and South. John Brown had set the nation on a course toward civil war.

Brown's actions caused a panic in the South that played into the hands of the secessionists. One Southerner wrote, "The Harpers Ferry affair . . . gives new interest to the question of disunion." As summer passed and the crucial presidential election of 1860 approached, speakers supporting secession made terrifying prophecies. If Lincoln and the "Black Republicans" won control of the federal government, they said, Northerners would invade the South and incite the slaves to revolt, murder, and rape. On the floor of the U.S. Senate, Jefferson Davis insisted that if the Republicans took control, "then John Brown, and a thousand John Browns, can invade us, and . . . the Black Republican Government will stand and permit our soil to be violated, and our people assailed and raise no arm in our defense."

THE ELECTION OF ABRAHAM LINCOLN

In 1856, John Frémont, the first Republican presidential candidate, came within a whisker of defeating James Buchanan. The Republicans felt they could win the presidential election of 1860. In order to do this, the Republican Party did not nominate William Seward, the controversial abolitionist from New York. Instead, they chose the more moderate Abraham Lincoln of Illinois.

Because the Republicans wanted to win the election, they tried to distance themselves as much as possible from Brown. Republicans condemned the raid and dismissed Brown as an insane, solitary fanatic who was justly hanged. One of Lincoln's advisers wrote the candidate, "The old idiot—the quicker they hang him and get him out of the way the better." Even Seward called the deaths of Brown and his followers "pitiable, although necessary and just, because they acted under delirium, which blinded their judgments to the real nature of their criminal enterprise."

Although Abraham Lincoln called John Brown a "misguided lunatic," Brown's actions and statements in prison and the courtroom helped ensure Lincoln's election as president. Abolitionists came to see Brown as heroic, while Southerners characterized him as a black-hearted villain. The raid on Harpers Ferry escalated tensions between the North and South even further, leading to the secession of the Southern states and the American Civil War.

Lincoln echoed his party's view. On the day after Brown's hanging, Lincoln told a Kansas audience that, "even though [Brown] agreed with us in thinking slavery wrong, that cannot excuse violence, bloodshed, and treason." Lincoln's important Cooper Union (New York City) speech, which helped get him elected, contained a section denying any connection between the Republican Party and Harpers Ferry. "John Brown was no Republican," Lincoln stated, "and you have failed to implicate a single Republican in his Harpers Ferry enterprise." He mocked Brown as "an enthusiast [who] broods over the oppression of a people till he fancies himself commissioned by heaven to liberate them." The platform of the Republican Party, written in the summer of 1860, stated, "we denounce the lawless invasion by armed force of the soil of any state or territory, no matter under what pretext, as among the gravest crimes."

The Republican strategy was successful. In 1860, Abraham Lincoln was elected president of the United States. He won a four-person race with about 40 percent of the vote. He won every Northern state except New Jersey.

FORT SUMTER

As a Republican, President Lincoln believed that slavery should not expand to the West. In his first speech as president in 1861, he specifically promised the South, "I have no purpose, directly or indirectly, to interfere with the institution of slavery in the States where it exists. I believe I have no lawful right to do so, and I have no inclination to do so."

Eleven Southern states did not believe him. John Brown's raid had tipped the balance of power and influence in the South in favor of the secessionists. Eventually, these Southern states decided to leave the United States and form their own country named the Confederate States of America. The American Civil War began in 1861, when Southern rebels attacked Fort Sumter, a U.S. fort outside Charleston, South Carolina.

John Brown's raid intensified the disagreements between the North and the South that helped to tear the Union apart. Alabama government advisor Anthony Dillard later wrote, "But for John Brown's insane attack upon Harpers Ferry it is very questionable whether any of the Southern States could have been screwed up and egged on to secede, purely because of the election of Mr. Lincoln."

"JOHN BROWN'S BODY"

The outbreak of the Civil War assured John Brown's status as a martyr. It was a song that gave him undying fame.

Early in the Civil War, a soldier named John Brown served in the 12th Massachusetts Regiment. The men in the regiment teased him by setting humorous words to a tune probably written in the mid-1850s by William Steffe. The words were intended as a joke on the soldier. Audiences assumed, of course, that the song was intended to honor the recently executed abolitionist John Brown. The rousing song became the favorite Union marching song during the Civil War. Men marched into battle singing "John Brown's Body."

John Brown's body lies a mouldering in the grave,
While weep the sons of bondage, whom he ventured all to save,
But though he lost his life in struggling for the slave,
His soul is marching on.
Glory, Glory, Hallelujah! Glory, Glory, Hallelujah!
Glory, Glory, Hallelujah! His soul is marching on.

Few songs in American history have had as great an impact as "John Brown's Body." During the Civil War, hundreds of soldiers and civilians added new verses. The words changed according to the singers and the situation, sometimes funny, sarcastic, mean, or ribald. In 1861, the poet Julia Ward Howe, wife of Secret Six member Samuel Gridley Howe, was visiting Washington D.C. She heard the song and was inspired to write new lyrics to the popular tune. Her "Battle Hymn of the Republic," published in the *Atlantic Monthly* in 1862, became an instant classic. She had known John Brown quite well, and in the song, managed to combine John Brown's Calvinist world-view with the North's mission in the war.

> Mine eyes have seen the glory of the coming of the Lord;
> He is trampling out the vintage where the grapes of wrath are stored;
> He hath loosed the fateful lightning of His terrible swift sword;
> His truth is marching on.
> Glory, Glory, Hallelujah! Glory, Glory, Hallelujah!
> Glory, Glory, Hallelujah! His truth is marching on.

"The Battle Hymn of the Republic" has become the unofficial theme song of the Republican Party. The lyrics also feature prominently in several of Martin Luther King's speeches. King's last public words were the first line of "The Battle Hymn of the Republic,"- "Mine eyes have seen the glory of the coming of the Lord."

"His Soul Is Marching On"

The beginning of the Civil War was probably what John Brown hoped and prayed would be the end result of his Harpers Ferry attack. Soon, Northerners were invading the slave state of Virginia singing the marching song, "John Brown's Body." The Civil War lasted four years and cost more than 600,000 American lives. Brown's prophecy had come true; the crime of slavery would never be purged from this guilty land except with blood. "They could kill him," Frederick Douglass commented, "but they could not answer him."

At the beginning of the Civil War, the destruction of slavery was not the Northern goal. Several states that had stayed in the Union—Kentucky, Missouri, Delaware, and Maryland—still allowed slavery. President Lincoln argued that his primary purpose was to save the Union, not end slavery.

Only three years after Brown's attempt to initiate a slave uprising at Harpers Ferry, Congress moved to free the slaves by passing the Second Confiscation Act. Although it did not end the legal institution of slavery, it led the way for Lincoln's Emancipation Proclamation of 1863, which freed slaves in territories not under Union control. The Thirteenth Amendment officially abolished slavery in 1865.

A combination of problems caused Lincoln to change his mind. In September 1862, he issued the Preliminary Emancipation Proclamation, a symbolic move that made ending slavery one of the North's main war objectives. By that time, many slaves had taken freedom into their own hands by fleeing to areas that were under Union control.

All slaves were not freed, however, until the Confederacy fell and the Thirteenth Amendment was ratified in December 1865. Therefore, the 4 million human beings enslaved before the war were free after it ended. Had there been no war, then perhaps slavery would have lasted for many years to come.

POSTSCRIPT

Five of the Harpers Ferry raiders escaped with their lives. Charles Tidd entered the Union Army in 1861. He died of fever in 1862 at the battle of Roanoke Island. Barclay Coppoc went back to Kansas in 1860, helped to rescue some Missouri slaves, and then served as an officer in the Kansas Infantry. He died when a train he was riding on fell into the Platte River from a 40-foot-high trestle; Confederates had burned away the trestle supports. Francis Merriam fled to Canada after Brown's execution. He later settled in Illinois and enlisted in the Union Army. Merriam fought with Ulysses Grant as an officer with a black regiment. He died suddenly in 1865.

Brown's son, Owen, was the only survivor of the raid who did not enter the Union Army. He moved to Ohio after the Civil War and became a grape grower. He then moved to Pasadena, California, where he died in 1891. He never married.

Osborne Anderson was the only surviving African-American member of the raid. For a time, he lived in Canada and gave lectures to abolitionist groups. He wrote an account of Brown's raid from his perspective entitled *A Voice from Harpers Ferry*. During the Civil War, Anderson served as a noncommissioned officer in the Union Army. He died of tuberculosis at age 41 in Washington D.C.

Salmon Brown, as well as his sisters Sarah and Ellen, moved to California during the Civil War. John Brown's widow, Mary, remained on the North Elba farm until 1864. She spent the last 20 years of her life in California, living with several of her children. Salmon owned a farm and raised sheep, grew some grapes and fruit, and raised a large family. He committed suicide in 1919 for reasons not connected to Harpers Ferry.

Forty years after the attack on Harpers Ferry, the bodies of eight of John Brown's comrades were removed from their crude graves on the bank of the Shenandoah River. The bodies were brought to North Elba and buried next to their leader. The bodies of Aaron Stevens and Albert Hazlett were also disinterred from their graves in New Jersey and brought to the North Elba farm. On a warm day in August 1899, 1,500 spectators gathered near the gravesite next to the granite boulder. Lyman Epps, now an old man, once more led his sons in singing Brown's favorite hymns.

THE METEOR OF WAR

In November 1859, while Brown was awaiting execution, a series of meteor showers dazzled American skies at night. Meteors have long been linked in popular folklore to wars and disasters. One huge meteor raced across the morning sky and then exploded with a blinding flash. This meteor could be seen as far north as Albany, New York, and as far south as Fredericksburg, Virginia. For many Americans, it seemed the perfect simile for John Brown.

"John Brown's career for the last six weeks of his life was meteor-like, flashing through the darkness in which we live," said Henry David Thoreau. "I know of nothing so miraculous in our history." Thoreau was not the only one who compared John Brown to a meteor. Walt Whitman, America's greatest poet, featured Brown in his poem "Year of Meteors." And Herman Melville, the author of *Moby Dick*, in a famous 14-line poem entitled, "The Portent," called Brown "the meteor of war." To Melville, Brown was a gloomy sign of the civil war yet to come. In fact, John Brown's attack on Harpers Ferry did play a leading role in the origins of the American Civil War. Brown's raid convinced white Southerners that secession was the only answer to retaining slavery. At the same time, Brown pressured uncommitted people in the North into taking sides.

Slavery was a uniquely immoral institution in the United States. The institution deprived millions of African Americans of their rights as Americans and their dignity as human beings. Yet the number of slaves kept growing from 1800 to 1860. It seemed impossible to eliminate slavery by democratic means.

Law, custom, and prejudice all worked to support it; the Dred Scott decision and the Kansas-Nebraska Act confirmed this for all abolitionists.

It was Brown's fate to break this deadlock. What seemed impossible in 1859 came to pass in 1865. Brown wrote from prison, "Christ told me to remember them that are in bonds, as bound with them, to do towards them as I would wish them to do towards me in similar circumstances." This combination of Brown's two favorite Biblical verses reminded Americans in the North and the South that, regardless of skin color, their fates were bound up in the fates of slaves.

JOHN BROWN IN LITERATURE AND ART

John Brown's life has been the subject of thousands of poems, novels, history books, songs, and paintings. One of the more famous works was an epic poem entitled "John Brown's Body," composed by Stephen Vincent Benét in 1928. The poem won that year's Pulitzer Prize for poetry. In his poem, Benét called Brown a stone, "to batter into bits an actual wall and change the actual scheme of things." Many works of historical fiction have featured Brown; in Russell Banks's novel *Cloudsplitter* (1998), the old man has to share the leading role with his son Owen.

Some very famous Americans have written biographies of Brown, including W.E.B. Du Bois, the great African-American historian and political leader, and Oswald Garrison Villard, the grandson of the abolitionist William Lloyd Garrison. In 1909, Du Bois and Villard helped organize the NAACP to fight for African-American rights.

THE RADICAL VISION OF JOHN BROWN

The Harpers Ferry raid was an extreme attempt to end slavery, but many white people supported that position. In fact, slavery would end in bloodshed only six years after Brown's raid. It was in his personal life, however, that Brown was truly unique. For everyone who ever knew him said that Brown was completely color blind.

Other white abolitionists also believed in the brotherhood of man and worked incredibly hard to end slavery. Most, however, shared the racial prejudices of American culture and frowned upon treating dark-skinned people as equals. Brown

African-American artists often chose Brown as a subject. Horace Pippin and Jacob Lawrence both produced an entire series of paintings dedicated to Brown's life. For Lawrence, who frequently painted famous African-American figures, the John Brown series would be the only time his main subject would be a white man.

In 1942, Harlem Renaissance poet Countee Cullen wrote "A Negro Mother's Lullaby." The poem depicted an African-American woman taking her child to visit Brown's grave in North Elba. The mother sings her child to sleep with these words of remembrance:

Hushaby, hushaby, sweet darkness at rest,
Two there have been who their lives laid down
That you might be beautiful here at my breast:
Our Jesus and . . . Osawatomie Brown.

was different. He treated African Americans he met on terms of complete equality, dignity, and respect. He worked with them, surveyed their lands, and made friendly visits to their homes. For a white American to see blacks as his social equals was, for its time, perhaps more astonishing than the raid on Harpers Ferry. W.E.B. Du Bois called Brown, "the man who of all Americans has perhaps come nearest to touching the real souls of black folk."

Osborne Perry Anderson, the African-American raider who escaped from Harpers Ferry, phrased it best. In looking back on the experience, what astounded him was the sense of fellowship he achieved in the company of the other raiders. He later wrote, "In John Brown's house, and in John Brown's presence, men from widely different parts of the continent met and united into one company, wherein no hateful prejudice dared intrude its ugly self—no ghost of a distinction found space to enter. . . . I thank God that I have been permitted to realize to its farthest fullest extent, the moral, mental, physical, social harmony of an Anti-Slavery family."

CHRONOLOGY

1800 John Brown born in Torrington, Connecticut.

1805 Brown family moves to Hudson, Ohio.

1820 John Brown marries Dianthe Lusk.

1826 Family moves to New Richmond, Pennsylvania.

1832 Dianthe Lusk Brown dies in childbirth.

1833 Marries Mary Ann Day.

1836 Family moves to Franklin Mills, Ohio.

1842 Declared bankrupt by court.

1844 Moves to Akron, Ohio; enters into business partnership with Simon Perkins.

1847 Meets Frederick Douglass for the first time.

1848 Acquires 244 acres from Gerrit Smith in North Elba, New York.

1851 Establishes all-black League of Gileadites.

1854 Kansas-Nebraska Act passed by Congress.

1855 Follows his sons to Kansas.

1856 **May 21** Free state town of Lawrence, Kansas, is sacked by a proslavery army.

May 22 Senator Charles Sumner assaulted by Southern representative in U.S. Senate.

May 24 John Brown goes to nearby Pottawatomie Creek, Kansas, and leads his men in committing the Pottawatomie Massacre, the murder of five proslavery settlers.

June 2 Defeats and captures a larger proslavery force at Black Jack Creek.

August 2 Brown's men fail to defend free state town of Osawatomie against much larger force; Frederick Brown dies in the battle.

1857 **January** Franklin Sanborn introduces Brown to the Secret Six; Travels throughout New England to raise money and weapons for struggle in Kansas.

1858 Organizes antislavery convention in Chatham, Ontario.

December Rides into Missouri and attacks two proslavery homesteads.

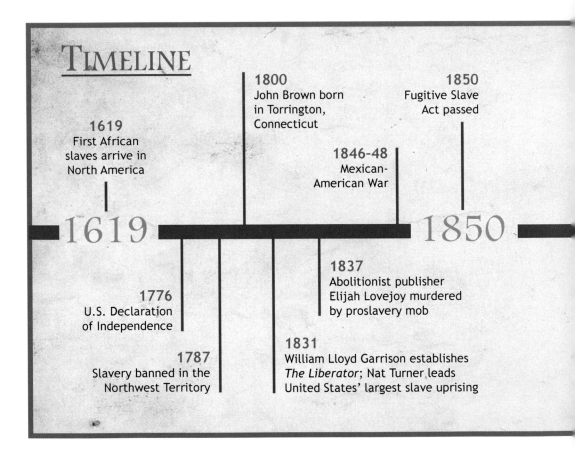

TIMELINE

1619
First African slaves arrive in North America

1776
U.S. Declaration of Independence

1787
Slavery banned in the Northwest Territory

1800
John Brown born in Torrington, Connecticut

1831
William Lloyd Garrison establishes *The Liberator*; Nat Turner leads United States' largest slave uprising

1837
Abolitionist publisher Elijah Lovejoy murdered by proslavery mob

1846-48
Mexican-American War

1850
Fugitive Slave Act passed

1859 **January–March** Leads liberated slaves on 82-day journey to freedom in Canada.

July 3 Rents the Kennedy farmhouse in Maryland, a few miles outside Harpers Ferry.

August 16 Secretly meets Frederick Douglass outside Chambersburg, Pennsylvania; Douglass declines to join raid.

October 16 Attacks the armory at Harpers Ferry.

October 18 Surrenders.

October 25–November 2 Stands trial in Virginia; jury finds Brown guilty of murder, treason, and inciting insurrection.

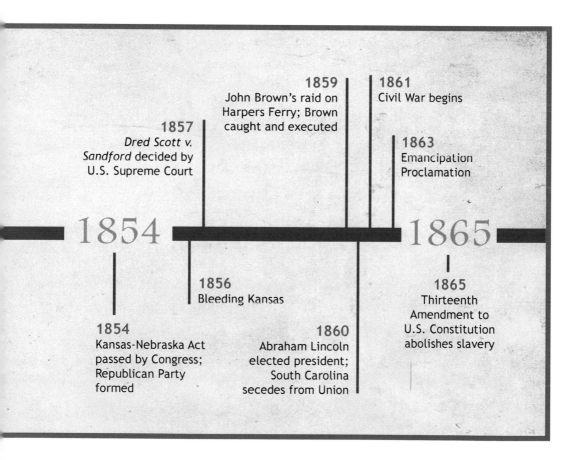

1859 John Brown's raid on Harpers Ferry; Brown caught and executed

1861 Civil War begins

1857 *Dred Scott v. Sandford* decided by U.S. Supreme Court

1863 Emancipation Proclamation

1854

1865

1856 Bleeding Kansas

1854 Kansas-Nebraska Act passed by Congress; Republican Party formed

1860 Abraham Lincoln elected president; South Carolina secedes from Union

1865 Thirteenth Amendment to U.S. Constitution abolishes slavery

November 2–December 2 Writes and answers letters from his prison cell.

December 2 Executed in Charlestown, Virginia.

1860 **November** Abraham Lincoln elected president.

December South Carolina secedes from United States.

1861 **April 12** Confederates open fire on Fort Sumter; first shots of American Civil War.

1865 Thirteenth Amendment to U.S. Constitution abolishes slavery.

GLOSSARY

Abolitionism　A movement to end slavery in the United States. Abolitionism flourished from 1830 to 1860.

American Anti-Slavery Society [AASS]　Abolitionist organization founded in 1833 by William Lloyd Garrison and Arthur and Lewis Tappan. The AASS had more than 150,000 members by 1840. Its members used speeches, literature, sermons, and petition drives in the fight against slavery.

Bleeding Kansas　A series of violent events between 1854 and 1858 involving antislavery Free Staters and proslavery "border ruffians" in the Kansas Territory. John Brown played a direct role in many of these incidents in an attempt to influence Kansas's entry into the United States as a free state.

Burned-over district　An area in central and western New York that was famous from 1820 to 1860 for its reform movements and radical politics.

Calvinism　A type of Protestant Christianity that stressed the idea that all people were weak and wicked sinners. John Brown was a Calvinist, although the movement was in decline in the 1800s.

cotton gin　A hand-cranked cylinder with metal teeth that removed the seeds from cotton fiber. Patented in 1794, the cotton gin led to the growth of cotton manufacturing and slavery in the United States.

Dred Scott decision　A U.S. Supreme Court decision in 1857 that ruled that black people could never be citizens of the United States even if they were not slaves. The Court also ruled that the U.S. Congress had no authority to prohibit slavery in federal territories. This decision meant that the Missouri Compromise of 1820 was unconstitutional.

Free Soilers   People who opposed the expansion of slavery into the territories of the western United States that were acquired when the Mexican-American War ended in 1848. Free Soilers were especially important in Kansas. They helped found the Free Soil Party in 1848 and the Republican Party in 1854.

Fugitive Slave Act   Law passed by the U.S. Congress as part of the Compromise of 1850. The law provided Southern slaveholders with unfair legal weapons to use to capture slaves who had escaped to free states. The law threatened the rights of free African Americans and was extremely unpopular in the North.

Harpers Ferry   In 1859, a small town in northwestern Virginia (present-day West Virginia) that was the site of an abolitionist raid by John Brown and his followers. A noteworthy U.S. Arsenal was located there.

Kansas-Nebraska Act   Act designed by Senator Stephen Douglass of Illinois and passed by the U.S. Congress in 1854. The Kansas-Nebraska Act created the territories of Kansas and Nebraska and allowed settlers in those territories to decide if they wanted to allow slavery within their boundaries ("popular sovereignty"). The act repealed the Missouri Compromise of 1820 and angered many people in the North.

Provisional Constitution and Ordinances for the People of the United States   Document written in 1858 by John Brown while he was staying at Frederick Douglass's house in Rochester, New York. The document created a government for a new free state in the area that Brown intended to invade. It was approved unanimously by a convention in Chatham, Canada, captured at Harpers Ferry, and used as evidence against John Brown.

Second Great Awakening   Christian movement that flourished between 1800 and 1840. Its supporters emphasized a very personal relationship with a friendly God. They believed that human beings have free choice in moral decisions. In many

areas, "camp meeting"-style preaching drew thousands of
people. The Second Great Awakening led to reform movements such as abolition, women's rights, and prison reform.

Secret Six   A group of six wealthy radical abolitionists—
Thomas Wentworth Higginson, Theodore Parker, George
Luther Stearns, Samuel Gridley Howe, Franklin Sanborn,
and Gerrit Smith—who agreed to finance John Brown's
antislavery activities.

Timbuctoo   A mostly black settlement in the Adirondacks,
founded by the abolitionist Gerrit Smith. Smith gave away
120,000 acres of his land beginning in 1846. He hoped the
Adirondack area would offer refuge to black families eager
to own land and flee the racism and poverty of Northern
cities. John Brown moved there in 1848.

Transcendentalism   U.S. literary movement that emphasized
individualism and critical thinking. The movement's two
most famous members—Ralph Waldo Emerson and Henry
David Thoreau—both supported John Brown's raid on
Harpers Ferry.

Underground Railroad   The system of secret routes used by
people escaping from slavery in the South and traveling to
the Northern states or Canada.

BIBLIOGRAPHY

Adirondack History Center Museum (Essex County Historical Society). *On the Trail of John Brown: What Mary Brown Saw, A Self-Guided Tour*, n.d.

Blue, Frederick. *No Taint of Compromise: Crusaders in Antislavery Politics*. Baton Rouge: Louisiana State University Press, 2005.

Boyer, Richard Owen. *The Legend of John Brown: A Biography and History*. New York: Random House, 1973.

Brown, Justus Newton. "Lovejoy's Influence on John Brown," *The Magazine of History* 23 (September–October, 1916): 97–102.

Cady, Edwin. *Young Howells and John Brown: Episodes in a Radical Education*. Columbus: Ohio State University Press, 1985.

Carton, Evan. *Patriotic Treason: John Brown and the Soul of America*. New York: Free Press, 2006.

Christian, Nicole. "North Elba Journal; Recalling Timbuctoo, A Slice of Black History," *New York Times*, February 19, 2002.

Copeland, John. "The Letters of John A. Copeland: A Hero of the Harpers Ferry Raid," Oberlin College. Available online at http://www.oberlin.edu/external/EOG/Copeland/copeland_letters.htm.

Cox, Clinton. *Fiery Vision: The Life and Death of John Brown*. New York: Scholastic Press, 1997.

Cullen, Countee. *My Soul's High Song: The Collected Writings of Countee Cullen, Voice of the Harlem Renaissance*. New York: Anchor Books, 1991.

Dana, Richard Henry, Jr. "How We Met John Brown," *Atlantic Monthly* 28 (July 1871): 6–7.

Decaro, Louis. *Fire from the Midst of You: A Religious Life of John Brown*. New York: New York University Press, 2002.

———. *John Brown: The Cost of Freedom*. New York: International Publishers, 2007.

D'Entremont, John. *Southern Emancipator: Moncure Conway, The American Years, 1832–1865*. New York: Oxford University Press, 1987.

De Witt, Robert. *Life, Trial, and Execution of Captain John Brown*. New York: De Capo Press, 1969.

Douglass, Frederick. *The Frederick Douglass Papers. Series One: Speeches, Debates and Interviews*. Vol. 3 (1855–1863). New Haven, Conn.: Yale University Press, 1985.

———. *The Frederick Douglass Papers. Series One: Speeches, Debates and Interviews*. Vol. 5 (1881–1895). New Haven, Conn.: Yale University Press, 1992.

Du Bois, W.E.B. *John Brown*. New York: Modern Library, 2001 [1909].

Earle, Jonathan. *John Brown's Raid on Harpers Ferry*. Boston: Bedford/St. Martins Press, 2008.

Finkelman, Paul. *Dred Scott v. Sandford: A Brief History with Documents*. Boston: Bedford Books, 1997.

———, ed. *His Soul Goes Marching On: Responses to John Brown and the Harpers Ferry Raid*. Charlottesville: University of Virginia Press, 1995.

Foner, Philip, and George E. Walker, eds. *Proceedings of the Black State Conventions, 1840–1865*, 2 vols. Philadelphia: Temple University Press, 1979–1980.

Garrison, William Lloyd. *The Letters of William Lloyd Garrison: From Disunionism to the Brink of War, 1850–1860* Vol. 4. Ed., Louis Ruchames. Cambridge, Mass.: Harvard University Press, 1975.

Harrold, Stanley. *American Abolitionists*. Harlow, England: Pearson Education Limited, 2001.

Hawkins, Hugh, ed. *The Abolitionists: Immeditism and the Question of Means*. Boston: D.C. Heath, 1964.

Hounshell, David. *From the American System to Mass Production, 1800–1932: The Development of Manufacturing Technology in the United States*. Baltimore: Johns Hopkins University Press, 1984.

Jeffrey, Julie Roy. *The Great Silent Army of Abolitionism: Ordinary Women in the Antislavery Movement*. Chapel Hill: University of North Carolina Press, 1998.

Le Beau, Bryan. *Currier & Ives: America Imagined*. Washington, D.C.: Smithsonian Institution Press, 2001.

Lerner, Gerda. *The Grimké Sisters from South Carolina: Pioneers for Women's Rights and Abolition*. Chapel Hill: University of North Carolina Press, 2004.

Ljungquist, Kent. "Meteor of the War: Melville, Thoreau, and Whitman Respond to John Brown," *American Literature* 61 (December 1989): 674–680.

Malin, James. "The John Brown Legend in Pictures: Kissing the Negro Baby," *Kansas Historical Quarterly* 8 (November 1939): 339–41.

McClellan, Jim. *Changing Interpretations of America's Past* Vol. 1. Guilford, Conn.: Dushkin, 1994.

McFeely, William. *Frederick Douglass*. New York: W.W. Norton, 1991.

Melville, Herman. *Selected Poems of Herman Melville*. Henning Cohen, ed. New York: Fordham University Press, 1991.

Monroe, James. "A Journey to Virginia in December, 1859," Oberlin College. Available online at http://www.oberlin.edu/external/EOG/History268/monroe.html.

Nudelman, Franny. *John Brown's Body: Slavery, Violence, and the Culture of War*. Chapel Hill: University of North Carolina Press, 2004.

Oates, Stephen. *To Purge This Land with Blood: A Biography of John Brown*. Amherst: University of Massachusetts Press, 1984.

Peterson, Merrill. *John Brown: The Legend Revisited*. Charlottesville: University of Virginia Press, 2002.

Phillips, Wendell. *Speeches, Lectures, and Letters by Wendell Phillips*. Boston: James Redpath, 1863.

Quarles, Benjamin. *Black Abolitionists*. New York: Oxford University Press, 1969.

Renehan, Edward. *The Secret Six: The True Tale of the Men Who Conspired with John Brown*. Columbia: University of South Carolina Press, 1997.

Reynolds, David. *John Brown, Abolitionist: The Man Who Killed Slavery, Sparked the Civil War, and Seeded Civil Rights*. New York: Alfred A. Knopf, 2005.

Robertson, Stacey. *Parker Pillsbury: Radical Abolitionist, Male Feminist*. Ithaca, N.Y.: Cornell University Press, 2000.

Ronda, Bruce. *Reading the Old Man: John Brown in American Culture*. Knoxville: University of Tennessee Press, 2008.

Rossbach, Jeffrey. *Ambivalent Conspirators: John Brown, the Secret Six, and a Theory of Slave Violence*. Philadelphia: University of Pennsylvania Press, 1982.

Russo, Peggy, and Paul Finkelman, eds. *Terrible Swift Sword: The Legacy of John Brown*. Athens: Ohio University Press, 2005.

Sanborn, Franklin, ed. *The Life and Letters of John Brown*. Boston: Roberts Brothers, 1891.

Smith, Merrit Roe. *Harpers Ferry Armory and the New Technology*. Ithaca, N.Y.: Cornell University Press, 1977.

Stauffer, John. *The Black Hearts of Men: Radical Abolitionists and the Transformation of Race*. Cambridge, Mass.: Harvard University Press, 2002.

Stewart, James Brewer. *Holy Warriors: The Abolitionists and American Slavery*. New York: Hill and Wang, 1976.

Tackach, James. *The Trial of John Brown, Radical Abolitionist*. San Diego: Lucent, 1998.

Walters, Ronald. *The Antislavery Appeal: American Abolitionism after 1830*. Baltimore: Johns Hopkins University Press, 1976.

Warren, Robert Penn. *John Brown: The Making of a Martyr*. Nashville: J.S. Sanders and Company, 1993 [1929].

Weber, Sandra. "John Brown's Family: A Living Legacy," *Civil War Times* (February 2005). Available online at http://www.historynet.com/john-browns-family-a-living-legacy.htm.

Wheat, Ellen Harkins. *Jacob Lawrence: American Painter*. Seattle: University of Washington Press, 1986.

Whitman, Karen. "Re-evaluating John Brown's Raid at Harpers Ferry," *West Virginia History*, 340. Available online at http://www.wvculture.org/history/jb11.html.

Whitman, Walt. *Leaves of Grass* (The 1892 Edition). New York: Bantam Books, 1983.

Wyatt-Brown, Bertram. *Yankee Saints and Southern Sinners*. Baton Rouge: Louisiana State University Press, 1985.

FURTHER RESOURCES

BOOKS

Altman, Linda. *Slavery and Abolition in American History.* Berkeley Heights, N.J.: Enslow Publishers, 1999.

Cohen, Stan. *John Brown: "The Thundering Voice of Jehovah. A Pictorial History.* Missoula, Mont.: Pictorial Histories Publishing Company, 1999.

Earle, Jonathan. *John Brown's Raid on Harpers Ferry.* Boston: Bedford/St. Martins, 2008.

McArthur, Debra. *The Kansas-Nebraska Act and "Bleeding Kansas" in American History.* Berkeley Heights, N.J.: Enslow Publishers, 2003.

McNeese, Tim. *Dred Scott v. Sandford : The Pursuit of Freedom.* New York: Chelsea House, 1997.

McPherson, James. *Battle Cry of Freedom: The Civil War Era.* New York: Ballantine Books, 1988.

Ruchames, Louis, ed. *John Brown: The Making of a Revolutionary: The Story of John Brown in His Own Words and in the Words of Those Who Knew Him.* New York, Grosset and Dunlap, 1971 [1969].

Sterngass, Jon. *Frederick Douglass.* New York: Chelsea House, 2008.

WEB SITES

A Plea for Captain John Brown by Henry David Thoreau, October 30, 1859: The Avalon Project at the Yale Law School
http://avalon.law.yale.edu/19th_century/thoreau_001.asp

Gerrit Smith Broadside Collection-Syracuse University Library
http://library.syr.edu/digital/collections/g/GerritSmith/
essay.htm

The Gerrit Smith Virtual Museum
http://www.nyhistory.com/gerritsmith/index.htm

Harpers Ferry National Historic Park
http://www.nps.gov/archive/hafe/home.htm

John Brown and the Valley of the Shadow
http://www3.iath.virginia.edu/jbrown

John Brown's Holy War. PBS: The American Experience
http://www.pbs.org/wgbh/amex/brown/

The Kennedy Farmhouse
http://www.johnbrown.org/toc.htm

Life, Trial and Execution of Captain John Brown; 1859:
The Avalon Project at the Yale Law School
http://www.yale.edu/lawweb/avalon/treatise/john_brown/
john_brown.htm

WWW-VL: Coming of the Civil War-1850–1860:
The Pre-Civil War Years in United States History
http://www.vlib.us/eras/war.htm

PICTURE CREDITS

INDEX

 ABOUT THE AUTHOR

JON STERNGASS is a freelance writer who specializes in children's nonfiction books. He has written more than 30 books; his most recent works are a biography of Frederick Douglass from this series and a history of Filipino Americans from THE NEW IMMIGRANTS series. Born and raised in Brooklyn, New York, Sterngass has a B.A. in history from Franklin and Marshall College, an M.A. in medieval history from the University of Wisconsin–Milwaukee, and a Ph.D. in nineteenth-century American history from The City University of New York. He has lived in Saratoga Springs, New York, for 16 years with his wife, Karen Weltman, and sons Eli (15) and Aaron (12).